True Love
VOLUME 1

True Love
VOLUME 1

A Biblical View of God's Love

RICKY LEE OHL

RESOURCE *Publications* • Eugene, Oregon

TRUE LOVE, VOLUME 1
A Biblical View of God's Love

Copyright © 2025 Ricky Lee Ohl. All rights reserved. Except for brief quotations in critical publications or reviews, no part of this book may be reproduced in any manner without prior written permission from the publisher. Write: Permissions, Wipf and Stock Publishers, 199 W. 8th Ave., Suite 3, Eugene, OR 97401.

Resource Publications
An Imprint of Wipf and Stock Publishers
199 W. 8th Ave., Suite 3
Eugene, OR 97401

www.wipfandstock.com

PAPERBACK ISBN: 979-8-3852-4261-0
HARDCOVER ISBN: 979-8-3852-4262-7
EBOOK ISBN: 979-8-3852-4263-4

VERSION NUMBER 03/10/25

Scripture quotations are taken from the Authorized (King James) Version. Rights in the Authorized Version in the United Kingdom are vested in the Crown. Reproduced by permission of the Crown's patentee, Cambridge University Press.

CONTENTS

About the Author | *vii*

Preface | *xi*

Introduction | *xv*

Chapter 1　　What Is God's Love? | 1

Chapter 2　　Creation | 18

Chapter 3　　God's Election | 27

Chapter 4　　1 John | 42

Bibliography | *59*

ABOUT THE AUTHOR

IN 1985, I RECEIVED as my Savior the Lord Jesus Christ (in Hb: *Yeshua Ha Mashiach*) and I experienced what is stated in the words of Jesus to be "born again." John 3:3 reads, "Jesus answered and said unto him, Verily, verily, I say unto thee, Except a man be born again, he cannot see the kingdom of God."

To elaborate, we (humans) may be considered in three fundamental components: (1) a physical body, (2) a soul (mind, will, and emotions), and (3) a spirit. We read in John 4:24 that God is spirit, and we are to worship God in spirit. But in our initial human birth, we were born in a body with a soul, which I will term the flesh, and began physical life, not a life in the spirit. We are all born into a fallen (sinful) world, in a fallen (sinful) state disconnected from God. But God made a way for sinful man to be declared righteous (acceptable to God) to enable us to be reconcilable to him. From our age of understanding, we all have a freewill choice to accept or reject the provision of God, to be regenerated spiritually and reconciled with God through Jesus Christ. Being born again is a spiritual birth through faith in Jesus Christ as Savior (in Hb: *Messiah*). To explain further this process of regeneration, when a follower of Christ receives Jesus Christ as Savior and Lord, they also receive the indwelling of the Holy Spirit of God (1 Cor 6:19). The Holy Spirit, who is also God is given to be, among other things, our teacher, comforter, helper, counsellor, and supernatural gift giver. In my case, within weeks of receiving Jesus Christ as Lord and Savior, I was baptized in water, which is prescribed in the Bible to be a public demonstration of our new life as a follower of Christ. From this point in my life, I have attended a church congregation or assembly (in Gk: *ekklesia*) and been exposed to various teachings and preaching from the Holy Bible, the Holy Spirit-inspired word of God. "All scripture is given by inspiration of God, and is profitable for doctrine, for reproof, for correction, for instruction in righteousness" (2 Tim 3:16).

As I have matured in the teachings of Jesus, a deepening hunger to receive revelation from God, of the deeper truths in his word and to experience, in greater measure, his presence and his empowerment, has grown in me. Through my seeking God and searching the Scriptures, I have come to consider and believe that the love of God is an important motivation for the Creator of the universe (in Hb: *Elohim*), the God of the beginning (in Hb: *Elohei Kedem*), to intervene in the lives of mankind and provide the Savior (Jesus Christ) for us.

> Beloved, let us love one another: for love is of God; and every one that loveth is born of God, and knoweth God. He that loveth not knoweth not God; for God is love. In this was manifested the love of God toward us, because that God sent his only begotten Son into the world, that we might live through him. Herein is love, not that we loved God, but that he loved us, and sent his Son to be the propitiation for our sins. Beloved, if God so loved us, we ought also to love one another. (1 John 4:7–11)

As we can understand from 1 John 4:7–11, God is love and he loves you and me. However, God is love; love is not God. Love originates from God and as we are created in his image, we can also receive and give his love. Accordingly, I consider that delving into the love of God is of great benefit to each of us and therefore love is a wonderful motivation for me in writing this book.

I attended Sunday school as a child and was exposed to religious instructions in primary school, but my born-again life in Christ did not begin until I was twenty-five years old. Two years after becoming a Christian, I was married to my wife (Yvonne) in 1987. Early in our marriage, I decided to focus my ministry pursuits, and I have a passion for music that exalts God, and this desire has never left me. In 1998, I graduated from a ministry college, in Christian Ministries and Biblical Studies. Then from 1999 to 2008, I completed three tertiary degrees, graduating in 2008 with a PhD in knowledge and argument visualization for wicked problems. My PhD research has been published in books titled *Knowledge Cartography: Software Tools* and *Mapping Techniques*. In 2018, I began to produce, author, and present a Christian radio segment titled *Thinking Right and Living Right*. Becoming a Christian did not bring about a life without trials. We read in Matthew 10:34–36:

> Think not that I am come to send peace on earth: I came not to send peace, but a sword. For I am come to set a man at variance against his father, and the daughter against her mother, and the daughter in law against her mother in law. And a mans foes shall be they of his own household.

However, as Christians, we are called to be ministers of reconciliation (2 Cor 5:18), and therefore Yvonne and I stand in the hope that every possible relationship in our lives will be reconciled with Jesus our Messiah.

Following Christ

From the beginning of my born-again life in Christ, I decided to follow Christ and sound biblical doctrine. Division by church denomination (apart from separation due to unbiblical doctrine and practice) is something that I have tried to avoid. Hence, throughout our Christian lives, Yvonne and I have been exposed to various denominations in pursuit of biblical truth and discipleship. These include Methodist, Presbyterian, Assemblies of God, Australian Christian Churches, Foursquare Church, Uniting Church Australia, and Australian Baptist Ministries. I will confess that there has been alignment with the biblical teaching of some more than of others.

ABOUT THE AUTHOR

As is biblically instructed, I am a born-again, water-baptized, Spirit-filled, Trinitarian follower of Christ. My relationship with God, the Holy Spirit, enabled discernment and the inspired words of the Bible from uncorrupted manuscripts are my guides in truth. Thus, through prayer, study, and comparison of biblical manuscripts and translations, I am confident in my preference for the King James Bible: Pure Cambridge Edition that was translated from the Masoretic Hebrew text and the Byzantine Greek Textus Receptus.

I also recognize that biblical Scripture is written in multiple forms, as God, in his omniscience has purposed. Most of the Scripture is literal (i.e., past, present, and future): history, science, law, governance, instruction for living, and prophecy. Some of the Scripture is parabolic, allegory, poetic prose, words of songs, and some Hebrew idioms. Importantly, every word in the Old and New Testaments is essential. The Holy Spirit has inspired every book, chapter, verse, and word. God provided only one true inerrant word of God, not multiple contradictory versions, and JEHOVAH preserves his true word eternally.

I also consider that the industry of biblical textual criticism, with its roots in the German Enlightenment (1650–1800), has done more harm in undermining confidence in the word of God than good. Undermining confidence in God's words, and sowing seeds of doubt, was Satan's strategy from the beginning. "NOW the serpent was more subtil than any beast of the field which the LORD God had made. And he said unto the woman, Yea, hath God said, Ye shall not eat of every tree of the garden?" (Gen 3:1).

God will and has always preserved his word for the genuine seeker of his truth. I have henceforth, aspired to obedience, in love, to "Study to shew thyself approved unto God, a workman that needeth not to be ashamed, rightly dividing the word of truth" (2 Tim 2:15).

PREFACE

OUR GOD IS PERFECT in all ways and is perfect always. He was perfect from eternity past and is perfect to eternity future. God is complete, unitary, and immutable (unchanging).[1] Nothing has been or will be taken from God's character ever. If he was not immutable, he would not be God.

The Bible records that God is love. The Bible also records that he is holy. He is full of grace. He is just and merciful. He is righteous and equitable. But contrary to some teachings today, God is also fierce with anger and wrath. He is jealous and he hates sin. And in all these God is infinite; boundless, immeasurable, and unchanging.[2]

God does not just do these things as we might, he embodies these things and there is no inequity in him. All these work in perfect wholeness in God. So, when he gives love, forgives sin, and offers salvation to sinful man or when he passes final judgment on a sinner, he is not conflicted. God is one, unitary God. He is perfect, holy, and righteous; therefore, his judgments are beyond doubtful scrutiny of created beings. While we live in this world, the Bible informs us that we see in part only and through a foggy lens (1 Cor 13:12). We perceive things through our limited understanding and point of view. But God sees all, and knows all, from eternity past to eternity future.

---

1. Tozer, *Knowledge*.
2. Tozer, *Pursuit of God*.

God does not change his mind or make mistakes because he is perfect. And this concept of perfection is impossible for imperfect creatures, like us, to fully comprehend. Comparatively, if a human judge makes a life-or-death decision, she/he will experience a conflict between justice and mercy due to imperfect equity or unity of body, soul, and spirit. Such conflict is not the experience of our holy God and, in fact, is impossible with God because his judgments are without fault.

Therefore, we will never comprehend God exhaustively as we are not of equal knowledge, intelligence, or moral standing. But one future day, in our glorified state, we will know him and ourselves more completely. Remember, to trust and obey is our only play. He is the potter, and we are the clay.

When the Bible records and informs us that God is love, we don't have a total comprehension of God's love because we are not him. But we can study these facts and what is more, God's word instructs us to do just that. We read in 2 Timothy 2:15: "Study to shew thyself approved unto God, a workman that needeth not to be ashamed, rightly dividing the word of truth."

Hermeneutic and Bible Translation

Firstly, in all things, I seek the leading and counsel of the Holy Spirit. The type of research, analysis, and writing that I present in this book series is guided by an interpretive methodology that I will refer to as expository hermeneutics. I have also applied my postgraduate expertise in grounded theory to develop conclusions. Regarding methodology, I apply principles of interpretation to exegete reliable and true biblical meaning from Scripture. I use expository hermeneutics to bring to light thematic meaning and follow that as it unfolds verse by verse, throughout each relevant chapter and book of the Bible. Furthermore, keeping biblical Scripture as principal aids in minimizing human bias. Accordingly, in the presentation of my analysis and discussion, it is necessary to include Bible verses. The Bible alone should determine Christian doctrine and practice. We must study the word, receive the word by heart faith, and live out the word in faith and love to experience its power and life.

Accordingly, the quality of the Bible translation used is critical. In my estimation, the 1900 King James Bible: Pure Cambridge Edition is the true word of God, a faithful English translation. Our English Bible, the word of God, was mostly translated into English by interdependent men of God, such as William Tyndale and Miles Coverdale. A large portion (80 percent approx.) of what is in English translations is found in the Tyndale Bible (1526), and for his efforts he was burned at the stake in 1536. Tyndale, an early Protestant reformer, who opposed restrictions on public access to the Bible, gave his life so that any English-speaking person could read the Holy Bible in their common language.

Nonetheless, I believe that in all matters concerning God's word, which was given freely by God, JEHOVAH, for the good of all mankind, his sovereign will, will be done. Accordingly, all Bible texts cited in this book are from the King James Bible: Pure Cambridge Edition (first published circa 1900).

INTRODUCTION

A DESIRE TO CONTINUALLY grow in my relationship with God has led me to seek greater revelation of the person and love of God. To this end, I engage in a prayerful, focused study of the inspired word of God.

> All scripture is given by inspiration of God, and is profitable for doctrine, for reproof, for correction, for instruction in righteousness: That the man of God may be perfect, throughly furnished unto all good works. (2 Tim 3:16–17)

> For God so loved the world, that he gave his only begotten Son, that whosoever believeth in him should not perish, but have everlasting life" (John 3:16).

The word "love" (including within the words loved and loves) is found in the New King James Version (NKJV) 546 times within 462 verses. For statistical purposes only, I refer to the NKJV because in the NKJV the Greek word *agape* is more often translated into the word love. And seeing that the topic of focus is love, these statistics are useful. *Agape* in the King James Bible is translated as charity in the books of 1 Corinthians, Colossians, 1 Thessalonians, 1 and 2 Timothy, Titus, 1 and 2 Peter, Jude, and Revelation (twenty-eight times over twenty-four verses). Hence, the word charity is only found in the New Testament, and possibly Bible translators were inspired to choose the word charity in these instances because it refers to love and action.

INTRODUCTION

The word love is found in twenty-nine of the thirty-nine books of the Old Testament and in twenty-six of the twenty-seven books of the New Testament. In the Old Testament love (including the words loved and loves) is found most in the book of Psalms (i.e., 45 times). In descending numerical order, it is then found thirty-six times in the book Song of Solomon, then thirty-four times in the book of Proverbs, then twenty-five times in the book of Deuteronomy, and then fifteen times in the book of Genesis. The next is thirteen times in the book of Hosea. The ten books of the Old Testament that the word love is not found in are 2 Kings, 1 Chronicles, Ezra, Lamentations, Joel, Obadiah, Jonah, Nahum, Habakkuk, and Haggai (see details in Table 1).

In the New Testament, the one book that the word love is not found in is the book of Acts. Yet God's love is evident in the book of Acts. Firstly, love is demonstrated by Jesus by sending the promised Holy Spirit to initiate the universal church, which would from then on incorporate Jewish and gentile nations. Also, with the person and empowerment of the Holy Spirit in believers, the universal church could then spread the gospel of Jesus Christ (God's love), without favoritism to persons or nations, throughout the whole world.

As is represented in Table 1, the word love is most recorded in the the Gospel of John, in which it is recorded fifty-seven times. The next in descending numerical order, the word love is found forty-six times in the book of 1 John. Comparatively, the Gospel of John has twenty-one chapters and 1 John has only five chapters, meaning that the concept of love is saturated in the short book of 1 John. The next is the book of Ephesians, which records the word love nineteen times. Then in the book of 1 Corinthians, the word love is recorded seventeen times, and in the book of Romans it is recorded sixteen times. Overall, there are sixteen books of the New King James Version in which the occurrences of the word "love" amount to double figures. See Tables 1a and 1b for the number of times the word love is used in the Old and New Testament books.

Table 1a—The Word Love

	Old Testament	# Chapters	# Love
1	Genesis	50	15
2	Exodus	40	2
3	Leviticus	27	2
4	Numbers	36	1
5	Deuteronomy	34	25
6	Joshua	24	2
7	Judges	21	4
8	Ruth	4	1
9	1 Samuel	31	11
10	2 Samuel	24	9
11	1 Kings	22	7
12	2 Kings	25	0
13	1 Chronicles	29	0
14	2 Chronicles	36	5
15	Ezra	10	0
16	Nehemiah	13	1
17	Esther	10	2
18	Job	42	1
19	Psalms	150	45
20	Proverbs	31	34
21	Ecclesiastes	12	6
22	Song of Songs	8	36
23	Isaiah	66	10
24	Jeremiah	52	10
25	Lamentations	5	0
26	Ezekiel	48	5
27	Daniel	12	3
28	Hosea	14	13
29	Joel	3	0

30	Amos	9	2	
31	Obadiah	1	0	
32	Jonah	4	0	
33	Micah	7	2	
34	Nahum	3	0	
35	Habakkuk	3	0	
36	Zephaniah	3	1	
37	Haggai	2	0	
38	Zechariah	14	2	
39	Malachi	4	4	
		Total	261	

Table 1b—The Word Love			
New Testament		# Chapters	# Love
1	Matthew	28	13
2	Mark	16	6
3	Luke	24	15
4	John	21	57
5	Acts	28	0
6	Romans	16	16
7	1 Corinthians	16	17
8	2 Corinthians	13	13
9	Galatians	6	5
10	Ephesians	6	19
11	Philippians	4	5
12	Colossians	4	6
13	1 Thessalonians	5	7
14	2 Thessalonians	3	4
15	1 Timothy	6	6
16	2 Timothy	4	6

17	Titus	3	5
18	Philemon	1	3
19	Hebrews	13	5
20	James	5	3
21	1 Peter	5	9
22	2 Peter	3	2
23	1 John	5	46
24	2 John	1	4
25	3 John	1	3
26	Jude	1	3
27	Revelation	22	7
		Total	**285**

The fact that the word love is found in fifty-five out of sixty-six books of the Bible highlights the importance of receiving, living in, and sharing God's love. Consequently, it behooves us to develop our understanding of God's love.

The statistics presented here are used only to draw our attention to the specific instances of the word (love) as a primer for further discussion. God's love is exemplified in Jesus Christ and is truly evident in every book of the Bible. Jesus is also evident in every book. King David in Psalm 40:7 and the apostle Paul in Hebrews 10:7 state, "in the volume of the book is written of me." This is a direct reference to Jesus Christ in Scripture. Meaning, that the coming of Jesus (past and future) and the redemptive work of Jesus Christ were recorded and thus foretold in the ancient Hebrew scrolls. Jesus is God and God is love.

Chapter 1

WHAT IS GOD'S LOVE?

THERE IS A DEFINITE MISMATCH between God's concept of love and one that is often communicated through our contemporary media and secular literature. Therefore, it is very important that I define the word love early in our discussion. In addition, I will mention that in the King James Bible: Pure Cambridge Edition translated from the Masoretic Hebrew text and the Byzantine Greek Textus Receptus, the word charity, also meaning love and its application, is often used.

The King James Bible: Pure Cambridge Edition uses Early Modern English also referred to in the Concise Oxford Companion as elevated Jacobean English (or Biblical English). Biblical English comes from a tradition of its own, evolving from the Wycliffite Bible translations in the fourteenth century. This form of English may sound unfamiliar to some, but one can be easily familiarized with it.

Biblical English includes the pronouns thou, thee, thyself, thy, and thine which are second-person singular, and ye, which is second-person plural. Accordingly, second-person pronouns are distinguished by their first letter; T-pronouns are singular, and Y-pronouns are plural. Verbs ending in "est" or "st" denote second-person singular, present-tense actions (e.g., thou lovest). Verbs ending in "eth" or "th" denote third-person singular, present-tense actions (e.g., he loveth).

Specifying first-, second-, and third-person points of view defines more specific detail into the intended perspective of the writer and textual context. Simply put, the first-person perspective uses I/we. The second-person perspective uses you. The third person perspective uses he/she/it/they. It can be understood by this explanation that the King James Bible: Pure Cambridge Edition language adds an increased level of precision in the translation that is necessary for Bible study accuracy.

Love as Defined in Modern Culture

Relational love in popular culture is represented by a strong emotional and mental state of a positive attraction toward an individual (or object). Love is often associated with an emotionally charged, romantic attraction, which is commonly contrasted with lust. Accordingly, love and infatuation are often conflated, characterized, and necessitated by an emotional feeling for another that wells up and might be sustained over a time that some might label as a honeymoon period. We can find many examples of the terms, love at first sight (infatuation), falling in love (overwhelmed by feeling), or falling out of love (loss of attraction). Thus, the degree to which an individual relies on the senses, on feelings of attraction and/or on romantic emotions will determine the longevity of "love" satisfaction in a relationship.

In contrast, biblical love is the outworking of God's love to each individual as we live by the faith of Jesus Christ. In Romans 5:5 we are told that the love of God is shed abroad in our hearts through the Holy Spirit, who is given to us. Hence, while the Holy Spirit dwells in us we can know and experience God's love continually and a focus on God's love for us can give us hope and uplift us through difficult times. As we receive God's love and give back to God our love, devotion, and obedience, we are built up (with the help of the Holy Spirit) to share our love with mankind. Furthermore, biblical love between a husband and wife is covenantal love as prescribed in Genesis 2:21–25 and as restated in the New Testament (Matt 19:4–6).

> And he answered and said unto them, Have ye not read, that he which made them at the beginning made them male and female, And said, For this cause shall a man leave father and mother, and shall cleave to his wife: and they twain shall be one flesh? Wherefore they are no more twain, but one flesh. What therefore God hath joined together, let not man put asunder. (Matt 19:4–6)

Biblical marriage is a covenant commitment between one man and one woman within which God directs us to faithfully love each other, for life. Biblical love is therefore dependent upon a continual act of the will to love, rather than a *reliance* on feelings of attraction and/or romance. To be clear, within a biblical marriage relationship, feelings of attraction and romance may exist and continue but we are to will or choose to love each other regardless of whether the feelings are or are not present. Furthermore, biblical marriage is the only relationship within which sexual intimacy is ordained by God and thus permissible and blessed by God.

God's Love in Us

God's love in us is revealed through us by our thoughts, motives, and actions. We display God's love and our love to him by our worship, honor, and obedience to him. Furthermore, God's love is perfected in us by our obedience to his word (see 1 John 2:5). Obedience to God's word means that we now live to serve God with all of our spirit, soul, body, strength, and mind, and we serve others with our God-given gifts and our good works. "But whoso keepeth his word, in him verily is the love of God perfected: hereby know we that we are in him" (1 John 2:5).

Contrary to some critics of Christian beliefs, the love of God outlived by us does not mean that we must approve or agree with another to show love. Our desire and ability to love others is an outflow of our primary relationship, which is with God, and that love is maintained and displayed through our obedience to his word.

The highest expression of love is self-sacrifice for the benefit of others. Jesus is the ultimate example of love, as he sacrificed himself unto death for everyone who will believe in him, accept his provision for redemption, and repent (change one's mind, purpose, and life) from their godless living and beliefs to faith in God. "And this is the will of him that sent me, that every one which seeth the Son, and believeth on him, may have everlasting life: and I will raise him up at the last day" (John 6:40).

Repentance

A side issue that I will address here is an argument by some that repentance is not an essential ingredient of salvation. I would submit that you cannot have salvific faith in God without God-honoring repentance, nor will you have God-honoring repentance without belief in God. There are many other references, but let's take a look at two Scriptures, Acts 3:19 and 2 Corinthians 7:10.

> Repent ye therefore, and be converted, that your sins may be blotted out, when the times of refreshing shall come from the presence of the Lord. (Acts 3:19)

> For godly sorrow worketh repentance to salvation not to be repented of: but the sorrow of the world worketh death. (2 Cor 7:10)

The Greek word used in Acts 3:19 that is translated into repent is *metanoeo*.[1] The meaning is to change one's mind for the better and to heartily amend with abhorrence of one's past sins. The Greek word used in 2 Corinthians 7:10 is *metanoia*, from the root *metanoeo*.[2] Therefore, it contains the same meaning but with a change of mind, as it appears to one who repents, of a purpose he has formed or of something he has done. *Metanoia* is used of true repentance, a change of mind and purpose and life, to which remission of sin is promised.[3] Therefore, I would consider that

1. Strong, *Enhanced Strong's Lexicon*.
2. Strong, *Enhanced Strong's Lexicon*.
3. Easton, *Illustrated Bible Dictionary*.

the plain meaning of the Scriptures above is obvious. They clearly communicate that repentance of sins is a required step in the conversion process.

That being said, the Scriptures are also clear that God demonstrated his love for all mankind in that while we were still sinners, Christ died for us (Rom 5:8). Accordingly, God has been, and is continually, reaching out to mankind to show his eternal love toward them and invite anyone who will to become reconciled with him through Jesus Christ. What is more, it is wonderful to consider the words of Jesus to his disciples in John 16:27, telling them that the Father God loves those who believe in his Son (Jesus) as Savior and Lord. "For the Father himself loveth you, because ye have loved me, and have believed that I came out from God" (John 16:27).

New Testament (Greek): Love

Bible commentators and scholars typically refer to four different Greek words that are translated into the English word "love" (*agape, phileo, storge, eros*). Each Greek word for love communicates a nuanced difference to the meanings communicated. The discussion following contains reference material from the International Standard Bible Encyclopedia.[4] To elaborate further, regarding the four Greek concepts of love, I will also include and discuss these concepts with reference to C. S. Lewis in his book *The Four Loves*. See definitions of the New Testament Greek presented in my map following.

---

4. Orr, *International Standard*.

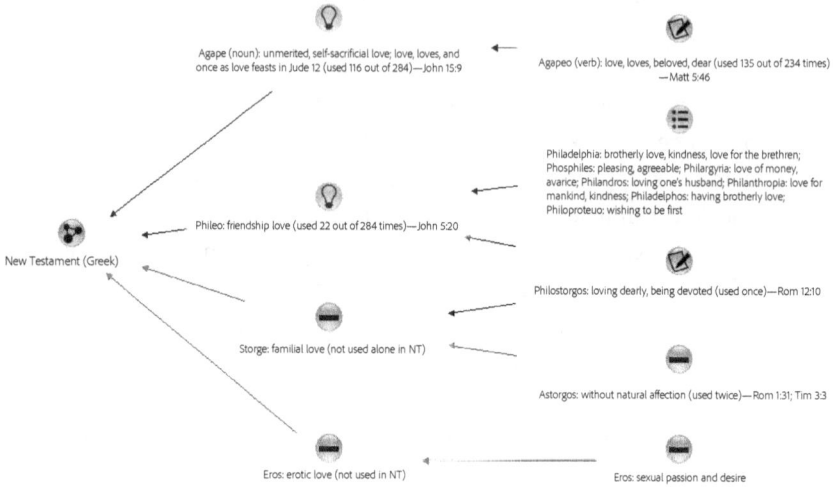

Agape—Unmerited God Love

Agape (noun form) and *agapao* (verb form) appear most frequently in the New Testament. Out of a total of 261 times where love is translated, 116 times it is the word *agape* and 135 times it is *agapao*. *Agape* translated as love (also charity) means to love undeservedly, despite disappointment or rejection. *Agape* is often viewed as God's love and an essential element of his nature. This unmerited, sacrificial love is what followers of Christ may express as God enables it as a manifestation of the Holy Spirit bearing fruit in the heart of a yielded believer. Christians are to express the unmerited love of God to his children and "to will the good of another."[5]

Agape love was shown to us by God first in his gift of creation and second in God's plan of mankind's redemption. God created us to be loved and to love. He first loved us and created us to love him and to love one another. In redemption, God showed his love for us by providing the only possible means to be reconciled to a

---

5. Aquinas, *Summa Theologica*, 1926.

holy God through the sacrifice of himself in human form, which is Jesus Christ. God took upon himself the sins of the world and paid the price to reconcile us back to him.[6]

> He that loveth not knoweth not God; for God is love. In this was manifested the love of God toward us, because that God sent his only begotten Son into the world, that we might live through him. Herein is love, not that we loved God, but that he loved us, and sent his Son to be the propitiation for our sins. Beloved, if God so loved us, we ought also to love one another. (1 John 4:8–11)

Agape love is, therefore, a gift from God to man and then expressed by man back to God. It is not given from a position of need. God loves with *agape* love because God is love. Furthermore, *agape* love is relevant to all the other love types that I will explain (*phileo, storge,* and *eros*) but *agape* love will and must be the primary love.[7] "Jesus answered and said unto him, If a man love me, he will keep my words: and my Father will love him, and we will come unto him, and make our abode with him" (John 14:23).

Phileo—Friendship Love

The next type of love I will discuss is *phileo*. From the 261 times love is found, it comes from the Greek word *phileo* twenty-two times. *Phileo* signifies the affection or attachment resulting in sentiment for someone (such as for a friend). Frequently, the focus is on close association. Of the four Greek love types discussed here, *phileo* love is the least of the natural or bodily forms of love. It is not circumstantial, nor is it due to an individual's function. It seeks not its own. An individual expresses *phileo* love because "he is he" and "she is she." Phileo love results in friendship that is deeper than companionship. For example, companions may come and go

---

6. Lewis, *Four Loves*.
7. Lewis, *Four Loves*.

but the loss of a true friend will impoverish us for life. Therefore, phileo love is long-lasting.[8]

> Charity suffereth long, and is kind; charity envieth not; charity vaunteth not itself, is not puffed up, Doth not behave itself unseemly, seeketh not her own, is not easily provoked, thinketh no evil. (1 Cor 13:4–5)

In John 21:15–17 we find a conversation between Jesus and the apostle Peter. It is interesting to note that when Jesus asked Peter if he loved him, there was an interchange between God's divine love (*agape*) and man's love (*phileo*). Considering that this conversation took place after Peter had denied Christ three times, prior to Jesus's crucifixion, we might deduce that Peter's failure led to a lack of confidence about his ability to express *agape* love back to Jesus. Yet Peter seems to be confident about his ability to express *phileo* love. Interesting to note, *phileo* love is not otherwise used in Scripture to express man's love to God.

> So when they had dined, Jesus saith to Simon Peter, Simon, son of Jonas, lovest [*agape*][9] thou me more than these? He saith unto him, Yea, Lord; thou knowest that I love [*phileo*] thee. He saith unto him, Feed my lambs. He saith to him again the second time, Simon, son of Jonas, lovest [*agape*] thou me? He saith unto him, Yea, Lord; thou knowest that I love [*phileo*] thee. He saith unto him, Feed my sheep. He saith unto him the third time, Simon, son of Jonas, lovest [*phileo*] thou me? Peter was grieved because he said unto him the third time, Lovest thou me? And he said unto him, Lord, thou knowest all things; thou knowest that I love [*phileo*] thee. Jesus saith unto him, Feed my sheep. (John 21:15–17)

There are several other words in the Greek New Testament closely related to *phileo*, translated into love that come from the roots (*phil, phila, philo*). These include four times from the word *philadelphia* (i.e., brotherly love, kindness, love for the brethren—see Rom 12:10); once from the word *philargyria* (i.e., love of

---

8. Lewis, *Four Loves*.
9. Unmerited love, loves, self-sacrificial love; also, love feasts.

money, avarice—see 1 Tim 6:10); once from the word *philandros* (i.e., loving one's husband—see Titus 2:4); once from the word *philoteknos* (i.e., loving one's children—see Titus 2:4); once from the word *philanthropia* (i.e., love for mankind, kindness—see Titus 2:4); once from the word *philadelphos* (i.e., having brotherly love—see 1 Pet 3:8); once from the word *philoproteuo* (i.e., wish to be first—see 3 John 9); and also, once from the word *prosphiles* (i.e., pleasing, agreeable—see Phil 4:8).

Storge—Familial Love

The next is *storge*. *Storge* refers to the natural affection one has for a family member, such as between a parent and child, between siblings, and between a husband and wife. *Storge* may also be used when referring to one's love for country or a sporting team.

Storge love has similarities with *agape* in that it is not puffed up, it suffers long, and is kind. But C. S. Lewis proposed that such paternal, maternal affection and/or our love for pets must be submitted to a higher power, otherwise, it may change into hate.[10] Accordingly, Luke 14:26 records the words of Jesus: "If any man cometh to me, and hateth not his father, and mother, and wife, and children, and brethren, and sisters, yes, and his own life also, he cannot be my disciple."

Storge love is a natural and/or bodily type of love. It develops organically and unnoticed through circumstances and familiarity. Thus, it becomes comfortable. It is not based on performance or status. It loves the unlovable and loves goodness (Lewis, 1960).[11]

In fact, *storge* is not used in the New Testament apart from a compound form (*philostorgos*) and an antonym (*astorgos*). The compound form *philostorgos* is used in Romans 12:10 combining *phileo* and *storge*. "Be kindly affectioned one to another with brotherly love; in honour preferring one another" (Rom 12:10).

---

10. Lewis, *Storge/Affection (Part 1/4)*.
11. Lewis, *Four Loves*.

The antonym (or opposite) of *storge* is *astorgos*, which means without love, without affection to kindred, and is found in Romans 1:31 (without understanding, covenant-breakers, without natural affection, implacable, unmerciful) and 2 Timothy 3:3 (without natural affection, truce-breakers, false accusers, incontinent, fierce, despisers of those that are good).

Eros—Erotic Love

The next type is *eros* from which we get the word erotic, meaning sexual passion and desire. *Eros* was not used in the New Testament. Greeks did not always consider *eros* to be something positive but rather something dangerous, an irrational form of love that could overtake a life. Any loss of control was a frightening concept to Greek thinking. The concept of erotic love (*eros*) is not directly addressed in the New Testament other than providing guidelines or boundaries for the sex within marriage. For example:

> I say therefore to the unmarried and widows, It is good for them if they abide even as I. But if they cannot contain, let them marry: for it is better to marry than to burn. (1Cor 7:8–9)

However, the Old Testament does address romantic love and therefore the concept of *eros* love. The Old Testament was written in Hebrew and not Greek but the Greek concept of *eros* love is well illustrated, for example, in the book, Song of Solomon.

> Let him kiss me with the kisses of his mouth: for thy love [*dowd*][12] is better than wine. Because of the savour of thy good ointments thy name is as ointment poured forth, therefore do the virgins love [*ahab, aheb*][13] thee. Draw

---

12. Dowd (or *dod/dode* [shortened]): from an unused root meaning properly *to boil*, that is, (figuratively) to boil; *to love*; by implication a *love token, lover, friend*; (well-) beloved, father's brother, love, loved one.

13. Ahab, aheb (aw-hab', aw-habe'): human love for another, includes family, and sexual; human appetite for objects such as food, drink, sleep, wisdom; human love for or to God; act of being a friend; God's love toward man; to individual men; to Israel; to righteousness.

me, we will run after thee: the king hath brought me into his chambers; we will be glad and rejoice in thee, we will remember thy love [*dowd*] more than wine: the upright love thee. (Song 1:2–4)

How fair and how pleasant art thou, O love [*ahabah*],[14] for delights! This thy stature is like to a palm tree, and thy breasts to clusters of grapes. I said, I will go up to the palm tree, I will take hold of the boughs thereof: now also thy breasts shall be as clusters of the vine, and the smell of thy nose like apples. (Song 7:6–8)

An individual expressing *eros* love will often stand by another regardless of difficult circumstances. *Eros* never hesitates to say, "Better this than parting. Better to be miserable with her than happy without her. Let our hearts break provided they break together."[15] *Eros* love may have a close association with sex, but sex can occur with or without *eros* love—although, without *eros* love, sex would be about sensation. With *eros* love, sex is about the beloved and pleasure is a by-product.[16]

Furthermore, Lewis proposed that the degree of seriousness towards sex is also a consideration. He argues that when sex is taken too seriously, it may become an idol.[17] Therefore, it should be approached with light-heartedness and playfulness.[18] Lewis cited that within intimate relationships, *eros* might result in naked bodies but within friendships, it may result in naked personalities.[19] He also added this qualifier—we need God's love to maintain all the loves.

---

14. *Ahabah* (a-hab-aw): a) love for human object; b) of man toward man; c) of man toward himself; d) between man and woman; e) sexual desire; f) God's love to his people; g) intimate friends and a father and child.

15. Lewis, *Four Loves*, 150.

16. Lewis, *Four Loves*, 136.

17. Lewis, *Four Loves*, 138.

18. Lewis, *Four Loves*, 150.

19. Lewis, *Four Loves*, 103.

How Does Jesus Define Love?

Next, I have included some Scripture references recording the words of Jesus, which might help us to consider the love that Jesus lived and taught. In the verses following, Jesus is instructing his disciples with a strong emphasis on love. We display God's love via a self-sacrificial love for each other.

> A new commandment I give unto you, That ye love [*agapao*] one another; as I have loved [*agapao*] you, that ye also love one another. By this shall all men know that ye are my disciples, if ye have love [*agapao*] one to another. (John 13:34–35)

> He that hath my commandments, and keepeth them, he it is that loveth [*agapao*] me: and he that loveth [*agapao*] me shall be loved [*agapao*] of my Father, and I will love [*agapao*] him, and will manifest myself to him." (John 14:21)

We display our sincere love to God when we choose to love Jesus.

> Jesus answered and said unto him, If a man love [*agapao*] me, he will keep my words: and my Father will love [*agapao*] him, and we will come unto him, and make our abode with him. He that loveth [*agapao*] me not keepeth not my sayings: and the word which ye hear is not mine, but the Fathers which sent me. (John 14:23–24)

Jesus has shown us by his actions, the love of our Father God and we are to continue to choose to show love to others and adhere to God's commandments.

> As the Father hath loved [*agapao*] me, so have I loved [*agapao*] you: continue ye in my love [*agape*]. If ye keep my commandments, ye shall abide in my love [*agape*]; even as I have kept my Fathers commandments, and abide in his love [*agape*]. (John 15:9–10)

In John 16, following, the Father loved the disciples with *phileo* love, which denotes long-lasting friendship and affection in response to their love for Jesus. "For the Father himself loveth [*phileo*] you, because ye have loved [*phileo*] me, and have believed that I came out from God" (John 16:27).

In 1 Corinthians 13:4–7, Paul gives us a detailed description of *agape* love. This *agape* is to be our goal and even to be sought above Spirit-given, supernatural gifts.

> Charity [*agape*] suffereth long, [and] is kind; charity [*agape*] envieth not; charity [*agape*] vaunteth not itself, is not puffed up, Doth not behave itself unseemly, seeketh not her own, is not easily provoked, thinketh no evil; Rejoiceth not in iniquity, but rejoiceth in the truth; Beareth all things, believeth all things, hopeth all things, endureth all things. (1 Cor 13:4–7)

Old Testament (Hebrew): Love

As the Old Testament was written in Hebrew, looking at the Hebrew words translated into love in the Old Testament can further enhance our understanding. The majority of times that the word love is found in the Old Testament (208 occurrences) it is the Hebrew word, *ahab*, *aheb* (pronounced aw-hab). This can mean human love for another (family, friend), including sexual (lover); human appetite for an object such as food, drink, sleep, righteousness, and wisdom; and human love for God and God's love toward man. Two examples of *ahab*, *aheb* in Genesis are 27:4 as love for an object and in 29:20 as a man's love for a woman. See definitions of the Old Testament Hebrew presented in my map following.

TRUE LOVE, VOLUME 1

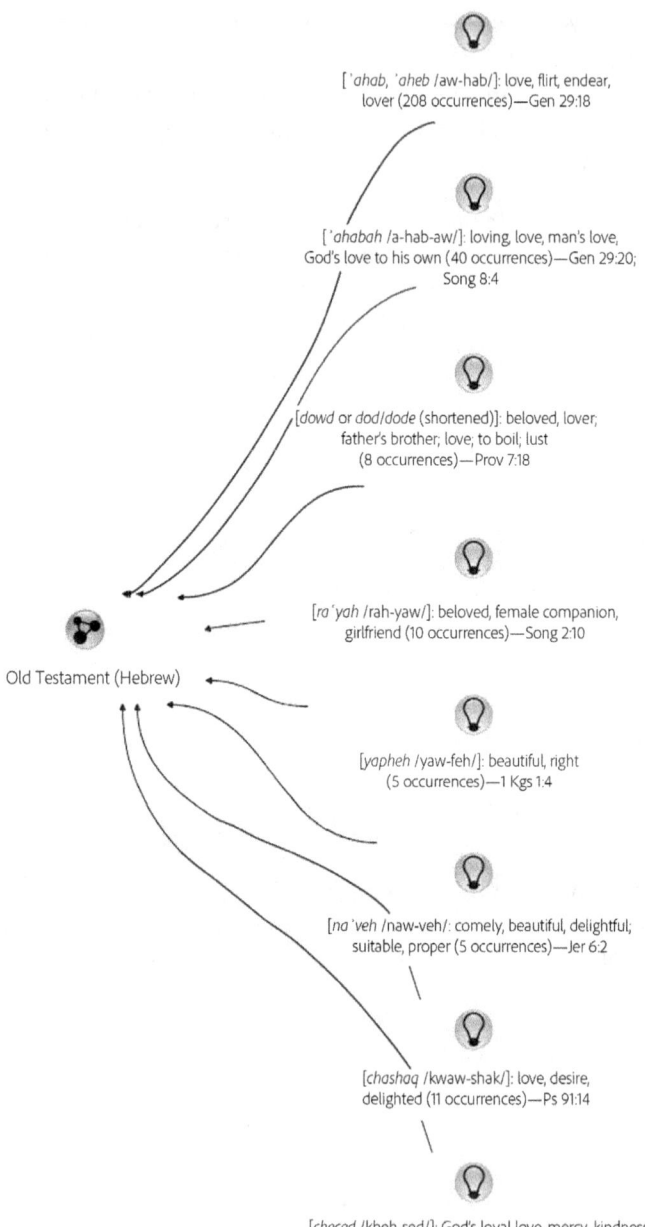

['*ahab*, '*aheb* /aw-hab/]: love, flirt, endear, lover (208 occurrences)—Gen 29:18

['*ahabah* /a-hab-aw/]: loving, love, man's love, God's love to his own (40 occurrences)—Gen 29:20; Song 8:4

[*dowd* or *dod/dode* (shortened)]: beloved, lover; father's brother; love; to boil; lust (8 occurrences)—Prov 7:18

[*ra'yah* /rah-yaw/]: beloved, female companion, girlfriend (10 occurrences)—Song 2:10

Old Testament (Hebrew)

[*yapheh* /yaw-feh/]: beautiful, right (5 occurrences)—1 Kgs 1:4

[*na'veh* /naw-veh/: comely, beautiful, delightful; suitable, proper (5 occurrences)—Jer 6:2

[*chashaq* /kwaw-shak/]: love, desire, delighted (11 occurrences)—Ps 91:14

[*checed* /kheh-sed/]: God's loyal love, mercy, kindness, loving-kindness, goodness (248 occurrences)—Jer 16:5; Exod 20:6

> And make me savoury meat, such as I love [*ahab, aheb*], and bring it to me, that I may eat; that my soul may bless thee before I die. (Gen 27:4)

> And Jacob served seven years for Rachel; and they seemed unto him but a few days, for the love [*ahab, aheb*] he had to her. (Gen 29:20)

As used in Deuteronomy 6:5, *ahab, aheb* refers to man's love to God. "And thou shalt love [*ahab, aheb*] the LORD thy God with all thine heart, and with all thy soul, and with all thy might" (Deut 6:5). In Ruth 4:15 we find another example of *ahab, aheb*, which in this context refers to the dutiful love of a daughter-in-law to her mother-in-law. "And he shall be unto thee a restorer of thy life, and a nourisher of thine old age: for thy daughter in law, which loveth [*ahab, aheb*] thee, which is better to thee than seven sons, hath born him" (Ruth 4:15).

In Deuteronomy 7:7–8, the Hebrew words *chashaq* and *'a-haba(h)* are translated to the English word, love. In these verses, referring to the Jewish people we read:

> The LORD did not set his love [*chashaq*][20] upon you, nor choose you, because ye were more in number than any people; for ye were the fewest of all people: But because the LORD loved [*ahabah*][21] you, and because he would keep the oath which he had sworn unto your fathers, hath the LORD brought you out with a mighty hand, and redeemed you out of the house of bondmen, from the hand of Pharaoh king of Egypt. (Deut 7:7–8)

God's love is often expressed in a metaphor of marriage. Throughout the Scriptures, *chashaq* is translated to mean desire, set his love, delight, in love, to love, be attached to, and long for.

The following are further examples of Hebrew words from the Old Testament that are also translated into English by the word "love."

20. *Chashaq* (khaw-shak): a primitive root; *to cling*, that is, *join* (figuratively) *to love, delight* in.
21. *Ahabah* (a-hab-aw): feminine, meaning affection (in a good or bad sense), love.

Come, let us take our fill of love [*dod*][22] until the morning: let us solace ourselves with loves [*o hab*].[23] (Prov 7:18)

As the lily among thorns, so is my love [*ra' yah*][24] among the daughters. (Song 2:2)

There are shades of differences in meaning between the Greek and Hebrew words that are translated into our English word love. There is, however, a consistent thread running through them. Orr notes that regardless of whether love in Bible Scripture is used about love from God to mankind, mankind to God, or relationships from mankind to another, it "is an earnest and anxious desire for and an active and beneficent interest in the well-being of the one loved."[25]

Another Hebrew word that is recorded a significant number of times (248) in the Old Testament is *checed*, pronounced "hesed." *Checed* is God's covenantal love and between humans it implies loving our neighbor with acts of love and service. Jesus's parable of the good Samaritan in Luke 10:30–37 is a wonderful example. There is no exact English equivalent. In the King James Bible, it is found 248 times and has been translated as mercy (149 times), kindness (40 times), lovingkindness (30 times), goodness (12 times), and kindly (5 times). The word *chesed* is used in every verse (1–26) of Psalm 136 and each time is translated as mercy. "Surely goodness and mercy shall follow me all the days of my life: and I will dwell in the house of the LORD for ever" (Ps 23:6).

This brief exploration of the word love, translated in the English Bible from the Old (Hebrew) and New (Greek) Testaments gives a technical overview of the various meanings, and thus nuances in the love God expresses. God's love to man (his creation), our love of God, and the type of love intended amongst mankind

---

22. *Dowd* (dod): to love; a love token, lover, friend; specifically, an uncle: (well-) beloved.

23. *Ohab* (o'-hab): affection in a good or bad sense; loved object.

24. *Ra'yah* (rah-yaw): beloved, female companion, girlfriend, attendant maidens.

25. Orr, *International Standard*, 1932.

are typically superior to much of what we find illustrated in secular society. In the following chapters, I will present a narrative of God's love as recorded within the biblical record (his words for you and I). The fact that God inspired every single word down to the smallest detail (jot and tittle) in the Bible to enable us to get to know him is another wonderful proof of his love for us. So let us proceed from the first book of the Bible, Genesis (Hb: *B'resheet*), which means in the beginning.

So What?

Love as represented in our modern culture and media is often not as God, who is the author of love, designed it to be lived and shared. God's love for each one of us has been demonstrated in multiple ways. Firstly, by the fact that he created us to experience and enjoy his presence, love, and his creation. Secondly, by the fact that he allowed us the free will to choose or reject him and his provisions. He also placed just, moral, and eternal consequences that will result from our personal decisions to reveal the truth of life with or without him. Thirdly, he provided a way of redemption via God becoming a man (Jesus Christ/Messiah) and dying a sacrificial death in our place to counteract the sin of fallen mankind and to meet all legal obligations for a righteous and holy God. Our part is only to accept his provision (i.e., the finished work of Christ) and repent (i.e., change our mind, purpose, and life) from a godless existence (sin) to a God-fulfilled existence.

The New Testament Greek and the Old Testament Hebrew languages are more expressive and exacting than our English. Within each of these we find a deeper expression of the word and concepts of God-given love. As we grow in our understanding and appreciation of God's love for us and in us, we can more closely live and experience the life that God intends for each of us.

Chapter 2

CREATION

BEGINNING FROM THE FIRST BOOK of the Bible, Genesis, we can identify God's expressed love. In Genesis, we read the record of God's creation. God created all that we can see in the array of wonders in the universe, and on the earth with mankind as the pinnacle of his creation. He also created all that we may not see, right down to the fundamental building blocks of material, such as atoms (protons, neutrons, and electrons) and, if real, the subatomic particles of quarks, hadrons, and bosons. We have also now uncovered intelligent design within the building blocks of genetic code, DNA (chromosomes), which are designed with unique hereditary information that instruct the growth and identifying traits of each living thing. God also created the unseen, spiritual realm of heaven and the host of heavenly creatures.

In the beginning, everything that God created was perfect. All of God's creation was designed to live in absolute peace and harmony with God and every element of his creation (the universe, the earth, and all life-forms) for eternity, but sin came into the world through mankind (Adam and Eve). Sin introduced death and decay into our world and sin was passed into the DNA of all creation, including all descendants of Adam and Eve. The concept of a finite lifespan, the deterioration of the material world, over time, and the deterioration of all life-forms have been scientifically identified and labelled as the second law of thermodynamics.

To recount the events that resulted in the fall of man and creation, we will look at excerpts from the book of Genesis.

> And the LORD God planted a garden eastward in Eden; and there he put the man whom he had formed. And out of the ground made the LORD God to grow every tree that is pleasant to the sight, and good for food; the tree of life also in the midst of the garden, and the tree of knowledge of good and evil. (Gen 2:8–9)

> And the LORD God commanded the man, saying, Of every tree of the garden thou mayest freely eat: But of the tree of the knowledge of good and evil, thou shalt not eat of it: for in the day that thou eatest thereof thou shalt surely die. (Gen 2:16–17)

Every element of creation was intended for our benefit and enjoyment but to provide a genuine choice by which we could demonstrate our love for God (or otherwise), God gave us choice and free will. Unfortunately, we failed in this first instance. We can also note that the warning not to eat from the tree of good and evil and the consequences were given directly to Adam, not to Eve.

> Now the serpent was more subtil than any beast of the field which the LORD God had made. And he said unto the woman, Yea, hath God said, Ye shall not eat of every tree of the garden? And the woman said unto the serpent, We may eat of the fruit of the trees of the garden: But of the fruit of the tree which is in the midst of the garden, God hath said, Ye shall not eat of it, neither shall ye touch it, lest ye die. And the serpent said unto the woman, Ye shall not surely die: For God doth know that in the day ye eat thereof, then your eyes shall be opened, and ye shall be as gods, knowing good and evil. And when the woman saw that the tree was good for food, and that it was pleasant to the eyes, and a tree to be desired to make one wise, she took of the fruit thereof, and did eat, and gave also unto her husband with her; and he did eat. And the eyes of them both were opened, and they knew that they were naked; and they sewed fig leaves together, and made themselves aprons. And they heard the voice of the

LORD God walking in the garden in the cool of the day: and Adam and his wife hid themselves from the presence of the LORD God amongst the trees of the garden. And the LORD God called unto Adam, and said unto him, Where art thou? And he said, I heard thy voice in the garden, and I was afraid, because I was naked; and I hid myself. And he said, Who told thee that thou wast naked? Hast thou eaten of the tree, whereof I commanded thee that thou shouldest not eat? And the man said, The woman whom thou gavest to be with me, she gave me of the tree, and I did eat. And the LORD God said unto the woman, What is this that thou hast done? And the woman said, The serpent beguiled me, and I did eat. (Gen 3:1–13)

Rather than face the responsibility for his personal indifference to God and disregard for God's warning of what would happen, Adam blamed God for giving him Eve, and Eve as the source of his misdeed. And Eve, rather than acknowledging her wrong, immediately blamed the serpent for deceiving her. In our present world, we are all faced with deceitful temptations to do wrong, but temptation is not a justifiable excuse for wrong choices and wrongdoing. Here, sin was demonstrated by Adam and Eve's doubting and/or disregard of God's words. Furthermore, the serpent purposefully inspired doubt of God's words and intentions. Conversely, love for God would have been shown by genuine consideration of and trusting totally in God's words and his holy nature. God can never lie, nor does he exaggerate or use his words carelessly.

> And the LORD God said unto the serpent, Because thou hast done this, thou art cursed above all cattle, and above every beast of the field; upon thy belly shalt thou go, and dust shalt thou eat all the days of thy life: And I will put enmity between thee and the woman, and between thy seed and her seed; it shall bruise thy head, and thou shalt bruise his heel. (Gen 3:14–15)

Accordingly, sin was the direct result of Adam and Eve's intentional disobedience to the simple instructions from God to not eat the fruit from a tree in the garden of Eden (the tree of the knowledge and good and evil). God warned Adam that if they were to eat from this one tree it would cause death and that is exactly what happened. Sin brought physical and spiritual death into the world. Once again, it is clear here that God allowed free choice regardless of the consequences, which expresses God's genuine love.

Genesis 3:15 communicates that from the outset of sin, God put into action a plan for the redemption of mankind, in order for us to be reconciled back into relationship with him. The enmity that God placed between Satan and the woman is the Savior, Jesus Christ. You should note, that in fulfillment of this prophecy, Jesus was born of a woman only, not a human man. The mother of Jesus, Mary (or Miriam in Hebrew), who was a virgin woman, encountered the Holy Spirit and was overshadowed by the power of God the Father. "And the angel (Gabriel) answered and said unto her, The Holy Ghost shall come upon thee, and the power of the Highest shall overshadow thee: therefore also that holy thing which shall be born of thee shall be called the Son of God" (Luke 1:35).

We can also see from Genesis 3:22–24 that after the fall had taken place, God removed Adam and Eve (mankind) from the garden.

> And the LORD God said, Behold, the man is become as one of us, to know good and evil: and now, lest he put forth his hand, and take also of the tree of life, and eat, and live for ever: Therefore the LORD God sent him forth from the garden of Eden, to till the ground from whence he was taken. So he drove out the man; and he placed at the east of the garden of Eden Cherubims, and a flaming sword which turned every way, to keep the way of the tree of life. (Gen 3:22–24)

The truth is that this was not done to punish man but rather for our protection. As I have stated earlier, from the beginning, all of God's creation was perfect and eternal and it is God's stated intention that he will make it perfect again. We can see God's reason in Genesis 3:22 for removing man from the garden at this stage. Within the garden of Eden, there was the tree of life; and the tree of the knowledge of good and evil. Eating the fruit from "the tree of life" would bring eternal life and eating the fruit from "the tree of the knowledge of good and evil" would bring death. If then Adam and/or Eve were to eat from the tree of life while in their fallen (sinful) state, they would remain in that state eternally and that (eternal degradation) would have been passed on to all their descendants. Consequently, seeing that Adam and Eve were the first humans, all of mankind descended from them. Therefore, the result would have been that God's plan of future restoration through a sinless savior, descending through Eve, would be thwarted. When we look carefully and prayerfully at each biblical account, we should always come to an appreciation that every decision of God is loving, righteous, just, and merciful. Every thought and action of God is a perfect expression of *agape* and *checed*[1] love.

Plan of Redemption and Election

In order to fulfill God's redemption strategy for mankind, he elected a nation (Israel) through which the Messiah would come and through whom the knowledge of JEHOVAH would be maintained throughout history. Through Israel came the law given to Moses, the prophets who spoke for God to direct that nation. These representatives functioned to record and keep God's word and uphold his ways and thus aid in establishing the conditions for the coming Messiah, Jesus Christ.

God Has Spoken by His Son

> God, who at sundry times and in divers manners spake in time past unto the fathers [Patriarchs—Israel] by the prophets, Hath in these last days spoken unto us by his Son [Jesus], whom he hath appointed heir of all things, by whom also he made the worlds. (Heb 1:1–2)

---

1. *Checed (kheh·sed)*: mercy, kindness, lovingkindness, goodness, kindly, favor.

God chose Israel and birthed that nation through men who had faith (trusted) in God: Abraham, Isaac, and Jacob (a.k.a. Israel). These chosen men and women of God give an example of the essential ingredient that mankind requires for reconciliation with God, that is, faith alone.

Yet, it is evident that the majority of mankind has rejected God's guiding hand revealed in his word (Bible), by his prophets and even by his Son. And Jesus is God's final offer and culmination for the plan of reconciliation for mankind. Jesus is the essential and foundational ingredient in fulfillment of God's plan and his ultimate act of love (sacrifice of his only Son). Even though Jesus was always with God and is God, the Holy Father chose to execute his plan utilizing and maintaining the freewill involvement of his elect (true Israel and true church): God and mankind in relationship throughout the history of the world to save all who love and trust God through faith in his Son (Jesus).

JEHOVAH, the Father, Son, and Holy Spirit is Lord and King over everything, but he has not domineered over mankind. The truth is that each and every element of God's design is governed by his perfect, holy being. Only perfect and holy love, justice, and mercy can proceed from him.

God did not introduce evil into our world but in his unsearchable wisdom and love he gives man free will to choose his good or Satan's evil. Furthermore, the spread of suffering in our world as a consequence of man's evil choices is experienced by all (faithful and unfaithful). Some will choose to seek God for help through such hardships; others will choose to blame God for their suffering and further distance themselves from him.

So then, we might ask the question: Why did God create his creation in the first place?

Everything that God created, the universe, the earth, all lifeforms including mankind, all declare his glory. The more we learn about creation, the more we discover the wonders of his work and identify the unmistakeable hand of God in all of creation. Psalms 19:1 and Isaiah 6:3 communicate this clearly:

> The heavens declare the glory of God; and the firmament sheweth his handywork. (Ps 19:1)

> And one cried unto another, and said, Holy, holy, holy, is the LORD of hosts: the whole earth is full of his glory. (Isa 6:3)

The Bible clearly represents, that amongst all of God's creation, mankind holds a primary position. We understand this from the fact that we were created in God's image; we were given dominion or rule over all of creation; and we were given the faculties to communicate with God, to praise and worship him and to make freewill choices.

> And God said, Let us make man in our image, after our likeness: and let them have dominion over the fish of the sea, and over the fowl of the air, and over the cattle, and over all the earth, and over every creeping thing that creepeth upon the earth. So God created man in his own image, in the image of God created he him; male and female created he them. And God blessed them, and God said unto them, Be fruitful, and multiply, and replenish the earth, and subdue it: and have dominion over the fish of the sea, and over the fowl of the air, and over every living thing that moveth upon the earth. And God said, Behold, I have given you every herb bearing seed, which is upon the face of all the earth, and every tree, in the which is the fruit of a tree yielding seed; to you it shall be for meat. And to every beast of the earth, and to every fowl of the air, and to every thing that creepeth upon the earth, wherein there is life, I have given every green herb for meat: and it was so. (Gen 1:26–30)

Consequently, mankind was invited to be in relationship with the God of the universe and to be his image bearers. God's choice of those who would place their trust in him and accept his offer of salvation through the atoning sacrifice and resurrection of his Son, Jesus Christ, demonstrates immeasurable love to his elect (i.e., those who embrace God). What is more, the fact that JEHOVAH gave mankind the choice to accept or reject him shows that he wants a true love relationship with us. Without the freedom of choice, our response to God's love would be forced.

God's Love and Provision for All

The genesis of our salvation is therefore motivated by God's gracious love and mercy toward each of us.[2] It is written in Ephesians 2:4–5 that God's wonderful love and mercy are toward us even when we are lost in our sins.

> But God, who is rich in mercy, for his great love wherewith he loved us, Even when we were dead in sins, hath quickened us together with Christ (by grace ye are saved). (Eph 2:4–5)

And it is an undeniable truth that God has provided the possibility of salvation for whosoever believes in him. "For God so loved the world, that he gave his only begotten Son, that whosoever believeth in him should not perish, but have everlasting life" (John 3:16).

In both the New and Old Testaments, we find examples of God's desire for all to be saved. In 1 Timothy 2:1–4 we are encouraged to pray to intercede and give thanks for all men to live godly and honest lives. That such supplications are good in the sight of God our Savior, who will have that all men come into the knowledge of him and be saved.

> I exhort therefore, that, first of all, supplications, prayers, intercessions, and giving of thanks, be made for all men; For kings, and for all that are in authority; that we may lead a quiet and peaceable life in all godliness and honesty. For this is good and acceptable in the sight of God our Saviour; Who will have all men to be saved, and to come unto the knowledge of the truth. (1 Tim 2:1–4)

> The Lord is not slack concerning his promise, as some men count slackness; but is longsuffering to us-ward, not

---

2. Orr, *International Standard*.

willing that any should perish, but that all should come to repentance. (2 Pet 3:9)

Have I any pleasure at all that the wicked should die? saith the Lord GOD: and not that he should return from his ways, and live? (Ezek 18:23)

Obviously, due to the free will of mankind, each individual has the right to accept or reject a relationship with God and unfortunately many do reject God's love, resulting in eternal separation and ultimately death. But God is not desirous that any man should perish. He patiently waits and his welcoming arms are open to all who will turn from their godless living. God has no pleasure in the death of the wicked (i.e., those intentionally apart from God) but his holy righteousness and justice can never be compromised by forcing anyone to accept his love.

So What?

God has demonstrated his love for all of mankind from the beginning of time and throughout history, up to the present and beyond. God is love and all that he does is an act of love. God had no desire that any of creation would be exposed to death and decay, but that man would make a freewilled choice to love, obey, and serve him and each other in love. Hence, creation demonstrates the wonderous beauty of God's design, but it presently falls short of the perfection of the initial creation and that which will come.

God created mankind in perfection and gave all the free will to accept or reject a loving relationship with him. Our federal heads, Adam and Eve, did reject God's offer to totally trust in him, which justifiably led to a separation from the holy God. Because of God's unchanging love for mankind, he put a strategy in place to pay the righteous debt for sin and to save mankind from eternal separation from him. Hence, mankind is offered the choice of redemption through the Messiah, Jesus Christ. Once again, righteous love dictates that acceptance of any offering by God to man is freely given. God's love permeates creation.

Chapter 3

GOD'S ELECTION

DISAGREEMENT ON THE INTERPRETATION and the theological application of the word election, as in the Bible, has led to a history of doctrinal division. Although, I do not intend to address all of the articles of this debate in this chapter or book, I acknowledge that there are various nuances within and around the topics of election, predetermination, and the foreknowledge of God. Election refers to who, predetermination refers to where (future destination), and foreknowledge refers to what and God's omniscience (knowledge of eternal events). However, election is important to a discussion about the love of God. Therefore, in this chapter we will explore the concept of election by God.

The Nelsen Bible Dictionary[1] defines the elect as a person or group chosen by God for special favor and for the rendering of special service to him. In the Old Testament the Israeli people are described as God's elect. In the Bible we read of Christ as God's elect, chosen of God (Isa 42:1; 1 Pet 2:4, 6), and the New Testament church as God's chosen people (Rom 8:33; 2 John 1, 13). Individuals are also deemed as God's elect according to the foreknowledge of God through the sanctifying work of the Holy Spirit to be saved in Jesus Christ (1 Pet 1:2; 1 Thess 1:4).

---

1. Lockyer, *Nelson's*, 331.

Election is the gracious, free act of God by which he calls those who become part of his kingdom through Jesus Christ and special beneficiaries of his love and blessings in relationship with him. Election may be considered in three different ways:

1. The election of Israel and/or the New Testament church as a people for special service and privileges (Deut 7:6; Rom 9:4; Rom 11:11; 1 Pet 2:9).
2. A person being chosen by God for a specific office or purpose, for example, Abraham, Isaac, Jacob, David, Solomon, and John the Baptist were all chosen by God for the positions they held; as were the twelve apostles.
3. God's choice of individuals to be children of God and heirs of eternal life (2 Thess 2:13; Eph 1:4; 1 Pet 1:2; John 13:18).

Election Choice

As with our choice to love one another, so too election here is a result of God's choice. The Hebrew concept of covenant love as expounded in the Bible is akin to our English word "choose." God chose us before the foundation of the world. He knows the end from the beginning (Isa 46:10). And because he knows us in advance (i.e., foreknows our existence, eternal thoughts, motives, intentions, and decisions), he predestined, calls, justifies, and will glorify those who will be conformed to the image of Jesus Christ.

> For whom he did foreknow, he also did predestinate to be conformed to the image of his Son, that he might be the firstborn among many brethren. Moreover whom he did predestinate, them he also called: and whom he called, them he also justified: and whom he justified, them he also glorified. (Rom 8:29–30)

God's Love for All

JEHOVAH loves mankind to the extent that he has provided the way to be reconciled (bought into relationship) with him. Reconciliation through faith in Jesus Christ is on offer to all. But this conclusion is doubted by some.

We read in John 3:16–17 that God so loved the world that he gave his only begotten Son in order that *whosoever* believes (has faith in God/Christ) should have everlasting life; and that he sent his Son into the world so that the *world might be saved* through Jesus. Also, in Romans 8:32: "He that spared not his own Son, but delivered him up for us all, how shall he not with him also freely give us all things?"

And again, in Hebrews 2:9: "But we see Jesus, who was made a little lower than the angels for the suffering of death, crowned with glory and honour; that he by the grace of God should taste death for every man."

Reconciliation in Christ

It is also of interest to me that once God has reconciled us to himself that he then gives the redeemed the ministry of reconciliation. But who is our ministry of reconciliation toward, if individuals have no choice in their salvation (i.e., irresistible grace)? And further, God has committed to believers the word of reconciliation, regarding that God through the atonement of Christ is offering reconciliation to the world.

> And all things are of God, who hath reconciled us to himself by Jesus Christ, and hath given to us the *ministry of reconciliation*; To wit, that God was in Christ, *reconciling the world* unto himself, not imputing their trespasses unto them; and hath committed unto us the word of reconciliation. (2 Cor 5:18–19)

My argument here is not to propose that all of the world will be saved. In fact, Jesus warns us and specifies that few find their way to life, as recorded in Matthew 7:13–14. Actually, why would

Jesus even bother to mention that few find the way, if all who are called will be saved?

> Enter ye in at the strait gate: for wide is the gate, and broad is the way, that leadeth to destruction, and many there be which go in thereat: Because strait is the gate, and narrow is the way, which leadeth unto life, and few there be that find it. (Matt 7:13-14)

Jesus the Door

My point is that the provision for potential salvation is available to all who call on the name of Jesus Christ. If this is not true, then Romans 10:9-13 is also in error and misleading.

> That if thou shalt confess with thy mouth the Lord Jesus, and shalt believe in thy heart that God hath raised him from the dead, thou shalt be saved. For with the heart man believeth to righteousness; and with the mouth confession is made to salvation. For the scripture saith, *whosoever* believeth on him shall not be ashamed. For there is no difference between the Jew and the Greek: for the same Lord over all, is rich to all that call upon him, For *whosoever* shall call upon the name of the Lord shall be saved. (Rom 10:9-13)

Accordingly, it is evident that apart from Jesus we can have no direct relationship with the Holy God JEHOVAH nor will he have a personal, intimate relationship with us. Apart from Christ we are unable to approach God as in our unredeemed, fallen, sinful state we are unacceptable to him. Yet, in Christ, we are redeemed and dearly loved children in God's family and can boldly approach him. When we are reconciled with God through Christ, we are among the elect of God and set apart for him.

God's Choice and Sovereignty

God has chosen us before the foundation of the world (Eph 1:4). He knows the end from the beginning (Isa 46:10). And because he foreknows us (i.e., our eternal thoughts, motives, intensions, and decisions), he predestined, calls, and justifies those who will be conformed to the image of Jesus Christ.

> For whom he did foreknow, he also did predestinate to be conformed to the image of his Son, that he might be the firstborn among many brethren. Moreover whom he did predestinate, them he also called: and whom he called, them he also justified: and whom he justified, them he also glorified. (Rom 8:29-30)

Considering this, one can understand that a personal, reciprocal, loving relationship can only ever occur between God and a saved, regenerated man/woman. God's truth is that he loves his elect (those in Christ) and extends an invitation to the unsaved. As we explored in the previous chapter, verses like John 3:16 ("whosoever will come"), 1 Timothy 2:4 ("desires all men to be saved"), and 2 Peter 3:9 ("that all should come to repentance") confirm this truth. If the offer of salvation is not available to all who will accept God's conditions, then these verses are in error. But they are definitely not in error and God cannot make mistakes or lie.

Furthermore, God extends his benevolent, merciful goodness to all of humanity, in that everyone can benefit from his various blessings of good weather and provisions in life, and his provision of salvation is on offer to all. However, outside of Christ, someone unsaved and indisposed to God will have no intimate connection with him. If an individual has not been accepted into God's elect through faith in Christ, they exist in the natural (i.e., the flesh) with a carnal mind. Romans 8:7-8 reads:

> Because the carnal mind is enmity against God: for it is not subject to the law of God, neither indeed can be. So then they that are in the flesh cannot please God.

Yet the goodness of God is further displayed in that even while we are at enmity with God (enemies), God (Jesus) instructs Christians to love enemies, and then we can be sure that he will abide by his own words and love those still in sin. Such benevolence, however, does not secure acceptance into the faith. But never overlook the fact that it is not God's desire for anyone to be lost (see 2 Pet 3:9).

Furthermore, it is a critical point to highlight here is that God's offer of salvation only remains actionable up to the point of our death. Beyond death our decision to either accept or reject, or any indecision, has permanently sealed our eternal fate.

In God's benevolence he has made provision for salvation for all who will come to him through faith in Jesus. John Wesley, the founder of the Methodists, purported that God in his prevenient grace also draws mankind so that, if willing, they will become disposed to seek God. Prevenient (or enabling grace) enables but does not ensure personal acceptance of the gift of salvation. Accordingly, it is God's desire for each man/woman to be reconciled to him through faith in Christ and to enter into a personal, loving relationship with him. Any rejection of God is maintained only by an individual's freewill choices.

Calvinism and Arminianism

The debate around election has been historically argued from the theological positions of John Calvin and Jacobus Arminius. While I do not intend to address these at depth, I will present them for context. While the authors of these theological ideas did not personally summarize their ideas into five distinct points, later adherents did. Arminianists first summarized five points around 1610 and Calvinists countered these in 1611 with their five points. In the table below, I have presented a concise summary of the points.[2]

---

2. Andrews, *Calvinism vs. Arminianism*.

	Arminian		Calvin	
1	Human Free Will	Although man is fallen (depraved), God enables the ability to choose him (a.k.a. prevenient grace).	Total Depravity (a.k.a. radical corruption)	Sinful unregenerate people, on their own volition, are unable to choose and trust God for salvation.
2	Conditional Election	God predestines people for salvation based on foreknowledge of their future acceptance of Christ.	Unconditional Election (a.k.a. sovereign election)	God chooses from eternity those who will be saved. Not based on foreseen virtue, merit or faith. Unconditionally grounded in his mercy alone.
3	Universal Atonement	Jesus bore the sin of all mankind.	Limited Atonement (a.k.a. definite atonement)	Only the sins of God's elect were atoned for by Jesus's death.
4	Resistible Grace	God can be resisted, and salvation rejected by free will (synergistic).	Irresistible Grace (a.k.a. effectual grace)	God's saving grace is only effectually applied to those he has sovereignly predetermined to save (monergistic). The purposeful inward influence of the Holy Spirit cannot be resisted by those God has sovereignly elected.
5	Preservation of the Saints	God works to preserve his people, but a person can fall from grace and potentially lose salvation through final apostasy.	Perseverance of the Saints (a.k.a. preservation of the saints)	Those sovereignly predestined by God to salvation, his elect saints, will continue in the faith to the end. Those elect who are not presently walking in the Spirit will be divinely chastened and will repent.

Comparison

Free Will

In Arminianism, a fallen and unregenerated person has an effectual free will to choose or reject God and is enabled by God to make this choice (i.e., prevenient grace), whereas Calvinism suggests that fallen man is totally distorted by the power of sin (spirit, soul, and body) which thwarts their desire and ability to effectively choose God for salvation.

Romans 1:20–28 is evidence that a fallen, unregenerate man has an awareness of God and as a result is held to account for her/his rejection of God (inexcusable).

> Because that which may be known of God is manifest in them; for God hath shewed it unto them. For the invisible things of him from the creation of the world are clearly seen, being understood by the things that are made, even his eternal power and Godhead; so that they are without excuse. (Rom 1:19–20)

Furthermore, the teaching in Romans 1:28 is that if such a person chooses to follow reprobate lusts and does not like to retain their knowledge of God (suppresses God's truth), God gives them over to a reprobate mind, leading to God's just final judgment. The principle here is that man has a choice and will be judged for making the wrong choice.

Election

In Arminianism the offer of salvation is available to all but the ultimate choosing by God (election) is conditioned on his foreknowledge that in the future, the person will genuinely accept salvation through faith. Furthermore, that redemption is based on faith in Christ alone, not on any personal virtue, merit, or goodness. Calvinism purports that God's election is God's sovereign choice alone, based upon his mercy alone and, similarly, not conditional on any merit on a man's part. Therefore, God sovereignly elects, without any involvement of a man's free will.

I would add that Romans 4:4–6 presents that salvation is not obtainable by a man's works but by God's grace (the source) and a man's faith in Christ alone (the condition). Hence, some in the Calvinist camp might argue that election is not based of man's involvement (a person's work), but it is clear from this Scripture that a person's faith in Christ is not a work.

Atonement

Arminianism claims that the atonement of Jesus Christ, his sacrifice, and thus payment for the sins of mankind was for all, the whole world (every individual), making salvation available to anyone who will accept his atoning work in faith (1 John 2:2; John 3:16–17); whereas Calvinism suggests that the atonement of Christ was done only for those whom God would sovereignly select for salvation.

I would add that by a plain reading of 1 John 2:2 and John 3:16–17, it is clear that the sacrifice of Christ was made for all people; not only for the apostles and the Jewish people but for the gentiles also, and thus all descendants of Adam.

> And he is the propitiation for our sins: and not for ours only, but also for the sins of the *whole world*. (1 John 2:2)

> For God so loved the world, that he gave his only begotten Son, that whosoever believeth in him should not perish, but have everlasting life. For God sent not his Son into the world to condemn the world; but that the *world* through him *might be saved*. (John 3:16–17)

Grace

Arminianism implies that the grace of God and the offer of potential salvation can be either accepted or rejected by an individual, whereas Calvinism maintains that God's grace is irresistibly applied by the Holy Spirit on those whom God has sovereignly chosen and, thus, these elected individuals have no effectual free will to accept or reject the salvation that is bestowed upon them.

I accept, without doubt, that God sovereignly elects for salvation unto glorification. Nothing apart from the grace of God has made redemption available for any one of us. Furthermore, God is the only authority on whom and why he chooses/elects and only God knows the true state of a man's heart and eternal future. No sinner and fraud will enter the kingdom of God as the holy presence of God/heaven, cannot ever be polluted with evil.

As I consider the various Scriptures pertinent to this topic, there are many that can be effectively and convincingly applied to either side. One must also acknowledge that it is easy to find and read Scriptures colored with a bias toward one side or the other. Both prevenient grace and irresistible grace require the sovereign gifting by God, and in both circumstances, a person's response would be foreknown by God. The distinction between these is one's free will to reject God's graceful provision—thus, fundamentally, a person's free will to choose God or remain in sin.

Regardless of the severity resulting from free will, it was a freewill choice that was afforded by God to our federal heads, Adam and Eve. We also find freewill choice given to the Israelites as recorded in Deuteronomy 28 (i.e., blessings or curses). And I believe that God's promises in Deuteronomy 28 of blessings for obedience or curses for disobedience extends to all believers. In Matthew 23:37, with reference to Jews in Jerusalem at the time of Jesus, we read that Jesus had desired to gather the rebellious, but they would not come to him. In Revelation 22:17, we read the final invitation to sinners, to follow Christ unto salvation. "And the Spirit and the bride say, Come. And let him that heareth say, Come. And let him that is athirst come. And *whosoever* will, let him take the water of life freely" (Rev 22:17).

Accordingly, I would argue that the principle of free will is demonstrated throughout the Bible and free will is illustrated by the nature and love of God. Grace is extended to us because God is love and he acts in love. Adam and Eve, nations, and individuals are awarded choice as this is a requirement of God's love. Without free will to reject, true love is compromised.

Salvation Security

Arminianism argues that it is possible, once it has been appropriated by God and an individual, for an individual to lose their salvation and become lost again. In Calvinism, the perseverance of the saints implies that an individual that God has elected to salvation, once saved, can/will never fall away from salvation—they will always persevere to the end (i.e., glorification).

I will suggest here that the word "lose" (their salvation) may be misleading. I propose that for an individual to depart from grace/salvation, it would require a conscious determinate freewill choice to reject salvation and/or denounce Christ. In Hebrews 5:11–6:12, we read the example of those within the body of Christ who were urged to demonstrate their faith by enduring in their commitment to Christ and not falling away. Hence, this is a warning about turning away from God (apostasy). The word apostasy means a public denial of a previously held religious belief and a distancing from the community that holds to it.[3] The inclusion of this biblical principle is evidence, to me, that God will not nullify the free will of a determined, unrepentant individual to depart from the faith (Heb 6:4–6). Without the ability (free will) to turn away, the biblical concept of apostasy is not viable and is redundant.

In Romans 11:21–23 we find an example of Israelites, from God's elect nation, referred to here as natural branches, being broken off because of their unbelief (i.e., the severity of God), which then opened the way for gentiles to hear and respond to the gospel and thus God gave them/us admission into the covenant promises to Israel (i.e., sovereign goodness of God). The condition for our continuing to be grafted in is for us to continue in his goodness, and if not, he will cut us off. Furthermore, when the Israelites turn

---

3. Koiter, "Apostasy."

from unbelief, they will be grafted in again—grafted in because of belief/faith, and cut off because of unbelief.

> For if God spared not the natural branches, take heed lest he also spare not thee. Behold therefore the goodness and severity of God: on them which fell, severity; but toward thee, goodness, if thou continue in his goodness: otherwise thou also shalt be cut off. And they also, if they abide not still in unbelief, shall be graffed in: for God is able to graff them in again. (Rom 11:21–23)

There is debate among biblical scholars as to whether this Scripture has national and/or individual application. Regardless, I would submit that salvation (or loss of salvation) can only be personal. I cannot be saved by someone else's faith in Christ, nor can I be cut off because of someone else's unbelief. I think that the warning by Jesus is also applicable here: "If a man abide not in me, he is cast forth as a branch, and is withered; and men gather them, and cast them into the fire, and they are burned" (John 15:6). Hence, abiding in Christ is expected.

Perseverance of the saints should be an intention for the believer and when one perseveres in Christ, glorification is guaranteed. In fact, I would also agree that confident assurance in our salvation is God's desire for all redeemed persons.

For the Arminian, preservation onto glory is protected by God but conditional on a believer persevering in their faith in Christ (abiding). Perseverance of the saint is an unbreakable rule, a proposed, foregone conclusion within Calvinism. Once again, in this last tenet, for the Calvinist, God's sovereignty overrides any possibility of a person's freewill choice.

Analysis

In each of these tenets relating to God's sovereign choosing (apart from free will), Calvinism certainly represents a salvation and sanctification process that is less complex, is more definite, and thus easier for man to follow (black and white). The inclusion of free will adds intractability into the mix, the ramifications of which are difficult for man to track and explain. However, complexity is not an obstacle for God who is truly sovereign, all-knowing (omniscient), and above the restraints of time.

From a personal perspective, I believe strongly in the sovereignty of God, but I find any lack of free will and thus imposed salvation to be contrary to Scripture and God's loving nature. In the eighteenth century, John Wesley stated that "God willeth all men to be saved, by speaking the truth in love." Why would God state that "He wills that all men be saved" or "who so ever believes in the Son will be saved," if he doesn't mean what he says?

For clarity, I wish to add a caution here that the propositions of universal salvation (i.e., everyone will be saved) and/or salvation via any other way than through personal repentance and salvation in Jesus Christ are unscriptural and anti-gospel.

My analysis of these positions leads me to agree with much of Arminianism. John Wesley also seems to counter some of the arguments with the concept of prevenient grace. Wesley purported that prevenient grace refers to natural conscience given by Father God to all men (John 12:32; John 16:8–11; Titus 2:11). Thus, Wesley believed that God's grace prevents the total destruction of the divine image in us. Furthermore, that prevenient grace is evident in the natural order of creation, in moral human conscience, in love for family, in decent human relationships, and in pangs of guilt for sin in unsaved individuals.

Man-Made Doctrine

Historical musings of men that have become traditional doctrine within the body of Christ are worthwhile analyzing, if not only to help in understanding the worldview of proponents. But God was not negligent in his choice of words in the Bible. The further we distance from actual Scripture to reliance on man's interpretation, the more disunity and confusion has occurred. The word of God is God's truth, and the Holy Spirit can, if we allow him, lead us into God's intended interpretation. Recorded in John 16:13, Jesus said: "Howbeit when he, the Spirit of truth, is come, he will guide you into all truth: for he shall not speak of himself; but whatsoever he shall hear, that shall he speak: and he will shew you things to come."

So What?

The elect of God is an important biblical term but has sidetracked many Christian discussions. Election, predetermination, and the foreknowledge of God are divine prerogatives of our all-knowing, loving God. God elected and set apart Israel as a covenant people, his representative nation, and birthed his word, his laws, and his Messiah through them, and has a future plan for them; he has chosen particular individuals (e.g., prophets, kings, apostles, teachers, etc.) and gifted them with divine gifts and purpose; and he grafted wild branches (those who are converts to Christianity from all gentile nations) into the covenant Jewish root (i.e., Abraham, Isaac, Jacob, apostles, and Jewish believers).

Election of God can be corporate and individual. Jesus Christ is the elect one and I believe that individual election is conditional on Father God's foreknowledge of one's faith in Christ, not on an individual's works, virtue, or goodness. In our election, in Christ, we are predestined to be conformed to the image of Jesus and adopted into the family of God. In election, the free will of man and the sovereignty of God are not compromised and we can know this because God is love.

I believe that I have approached this topic with an open mind, willing to allow the Bible to be the final arbiter. Accordingly, in my analysis, Calvinism prominently rejects the free will of mankind and in my understanding of Scripture and the nature of God, this cannot be reconciled with divine love. No doubt, clearly the Bible teaches that God is totally sovereign in all of creation and life, and he will be glorified in and by all. God both chooses and predestines his elect but also man has free will to accept or reject Christ. Regarding the concepts of God's sovereignty and our free will, in these, both God and man have a choice, and if there are some nuances of this that we don't fully comprehend yet, they will be revealed in God's time. Therefore, for me, and many others, by a plain reading and interpretation of Scripture, the general tenets of Arminianism, as presented in this chapter, can be reconciled with God's love and the biblical account.

Chapter 4

1 JOHN

THE SMALL BOOK OF 1 JOHN records the second highest number (46) of the word love within the sixty-six books of the bible. Therefore, I consider this book to be a good point on which to continue my discussion of God's love. In this chapter, I have begun with a brief outline of the book of 1 John.

A Brief Outline of 1 John

Many scholars agree that 1 John was written by the apostle John—the beloved apostle. An underlying purpose for the book was to promote fellowship (1:3), explain God's nature (1:5; 2:29; 4:7–8), and address a number of false teachings (heresies) in regard to false teachings about the deity and nature of Jesus Christ. These falsehoods would lead to immorality, which would lead to idolatry and eternal death, whereas God's truth will demonstrate itself in love and eternal life.[1]

There were three primary heretical teachings: Gnosticism, Docetism, and Cerinthianism. Gnosticism became a fully developed theological system by the middle of the second century. It was a teaching that combined eastern mysticism with Greek dualism (claiming that the spirit is completely good, but matter is

---

1. Radmacher et al., *NKJV Study Bible*.

evil). Based on this heretical teaching, some concluded that if God was truly good, he could not have created the universe. Therefore, some lesser god created it, the God of the Old Testament. The dualistic view (also Docetism) was that Jesus did not have a physical body but only appeared to have one and, therefore, did not suffer pain and death on the cross.[2]

Another heresy at Ephesus was Cerinthianism. This false teaching proposed that Jesus was only a man up to his baptism at which time Christ descended upon him but then departed from him just before the crucifixion, thus, purporting that the spiritual Christ did not truly suffer nor die for humanity's sins on the cross.

The biblical truth and corresponding firsthand accounts from those who physically lived with Jesus, including the apostle John, is that Jesus Christ is completely God and completely human. In this epistle, the Holy Spirit through John is promoting Christian unity, and thus for believers to live as God intends, in true love and fellowship, we need to understand the holy nature of God and guard against false doctrines.

God's Love in 1 John

In the following discussion, I have identified the Scripture verses in 1 John that include the word love and will expound on them around this central concept. Within these verses, there are only two Greek words used for love, the noun *agape* and the verb *agapao*, both of which I introduced in chapter 1. I have identified that these verses can be grouped: love perfected in us by his word, our love for God's word, our love for each other, believers set apart for God, God's love, his love in believers, and his assurance of salvation.

Love Perfected in Us by Keeping His Word

To begin, through my exposition of 1 John, I found that the word of God is a major source for growth in the knowledge of God and

---

2. Radmacher et al., *NKJV Study Bible*.

inspirational in learning of God's love and its applications. Accordingly, studying and living within the bounds of God's word is critical for experiencing, maturing in, and sharing God's love. "But whoso keepeth his word, in him verily is the love of God perfected: hereby know we that we are in him" (1 John 2:5).

Beginning from 1 John 2:5, we read that God perfects (i.e., completes, matures) his love in us by our application of and obedience to his word (also commands). The Bible is the life-giving word of God, which God has provided and preserved for us (Ps 12:6–7). As we apply his word by faith and deed we mature into the image of Jesus Christ. The Greek word for love recorded in this verse is the noun *agape*. *Agape* here refers to an affectionate and/or brotherly love. This love type implies that we would have the best interests for the welfare of the person who is the object of our love, and we apply this love in charitable actions. As you, a believer, pursues fellowship with God in obedience to his word the love of God matures in you. Maturity is then expressed by our love for others, our love for God, and God's love in us. In the verse following (1 John 2:6), John refers to abiding in God and how, when believers abide, our knowledge grows through experience of being in God. Brown et al. made the observation that in proportion to our love for God do we know him and by extent of this relationship do we attain full maturity.[3] It is a wonderful thing to know that God is with us always and directs our steps as we look to him, and that he seeks and enables love to grow in us.

Love for God's Word

As a consequence of studying and living in accordance with God's word, you will find that your love and appreciation for God's word increases. Hunger for more of God's word is a wonderful position to find yourself in and it will not disappoint. "By this we know that we love the children of God, when we love God, and keep his commandments" (1 John 5:2).

---

3. Brown et al., *Commentary*.

In 1 John 5:2 the Greek word for love is the verb *apagao*. *Apagao* means to love in a social or moral sense; to be fond of and to love people dearly. This can also mean to welcome and to entertain. Verse 5:1 relates to our faith in Christ, and by our love for Jesus, we demonstrate our love for Father God. In verse 5:2, we see that our obedience to God's commands displays our love for God and our propensity to love God's people. Accordingly, our love for God's people is proof that we love God.[4] "For this is the love of God, that we keep his commandments: and his commandments are not grievous" (1 John 5:3).

In 1 John 5:3, the Greek word *agape* is specific to God's love. As we walk out our faith and draw closer to God through obedience to his word, we realize that God enables us to overcome the temptations that would draw us from him. Our faith in Jesus is our source of strength in overcoming the sinful world. God's commandments should not be burdensome but also received as in love from God for our benefit. Everything from God, and back to God, should be fuelled by love, gifted in love, and received in love. As we can obviously see, love is a critical key for our life of faith and our ongoing sanctification (i.e., becoming like Christ).

Love for Believers

The next area of discussion is love for believers—those within the family of God. I will use the words one another, brother and/or sister, and/or man interchangeably to refer to individuals within the body of Christ. Our love and charity for believers is a crucial element of our life in Christ. I would suggest that this needs to be on display for all to see. In fact, when we withhold love from one another, God will chasten us to mature us in outliving our Christian faith (i.e., our Christian faith walk). "He that loveth (*agapao*) his brother abideth in the light, and there is none occasion of stumbling in him" (1 John 2:10).

---

4. Clarke, *Adam Clarke's Commentary*.

In 1 John 3:11, John acknowledges that the command to love our brother is not a new command but is fundamental and pertinent to our faith walk. As we are obedient to this command, we are living as we should as followers of Christ and walking in the light of his word. God's light reveals our way and/or obstacles that we need to avoid in relationships. As we continue in our love for Christ and love for others, we are prevented from giving and receiving justifiable offence. In truth, enlightenment comes from the word of God, not from man's so-called wisdom. "For this is the message that ye have heard from the beginning, that we should love (*agapao*) one another" (1 John 3:11).

God so loves us believers that he adopts each one of us into his family. Hence, we have become the sons/daughters of God, which is a difficult thing to fully comprehend. We were so far away from the holy God, irreconcilable, but God made a way through Jesus. Pure and sinless Jesus is the only provision we can look to, to cleanse us from sin. We are then to abide in him and live as he lives. Loving one another as Jesus loves us is an unchanging biblical teaching. It is recorded that in the latter years of the apostle John, when he was too old to preach, that he would say, "little children, love one another"; "it is the Lord's command"; "and if this is done, it is enough."[5] "We know that we have passed from death unto life, because we love (*agapao*) the brethren. He that loveth (*agapao*) not his brother abideth in death" (1 John 3:14). Now the love for the brethren (i.e., family of God) is a supernatural enablement from God. Yet, we are cautioned to walk as Jesus does, not as the sinful world does. We are to continually reject the temptations to stray from the ways of Christ. Unfortunately, when we cast off the likeness of sinful man, we will be hated by them, as Jesus was and is still. Accordingly, our love for believers displays evidence that we have moved on from our old, unredeemed life to our new, born-again life in Christ.[6] "Hereby perceive we the love (*agape*) of God, because he laid down his life for us: and we ought to lay down our lives for the brethren" (1 John 3:16).

5. Kirkpatrick, *Cambridge Bible*.
6. Radmacher et al., *NKJV Study Bible*.

We know that we have passed from the kingdom of darkness into the kingdom of light by the evidence of our genuine love for the family of God. We need no longer to be ruled by the prince of this world (Satan) because we now belong to the kingdom of the Prince of Peace (i.e., Jesus Christ). We have changed our position and now need to ensure that our allegiances align. The darkness inherent in the fallen world was demonstrated in the murder of Abel by his brother Cain (Gen 4:1–16). If we live in such darkness and hate our brethren, we are not walking in the light nor in the love of God.

Conversely, rather than taking life, even by thought (hateful), Jesus gives life to those who come to him for redemption. In the sacrifice of Christ, there is no higher example of true love toward a brother. Thus, from Christ's example we can conceive what true love looks like (1 John 3:16). "But whoso hath this worlds good, and seeth his brother have need, and shutteth up his bowels of compassion from him, how dwelleth the love (*agape*) of God in him?" (1 John 3:17).

Once again, here in 1 John 3:17, the apostle John is emphasizing love accompanied by action. If we are in a position of having the materials to sustain life (world's goods), then we can demonstrate sacrificial love, as did Christ, by giving to others in need. In comparison, this is an easier thing to do, than to lay down our life for another. If we are not sympathetic and charitable to the needy (especially the family of God), our profession of faith is insincere. "Beloved, let us love (*agapao*) one another: for love (*agape*) is of God; and every one that loveth (*agapao*) is born of God, and knoweth God" (1 John 4:7).

Righteous love is charitable and promotes the welfare of another in both a material and spiritual sense. The anti-Christian spirit is selfish, and makes one's own interests, intellect, and self-satisfaction the measure of achievement.[7] As God is love, his love shown in and through us is proof that we are partakers of his divine nature and that we know him (2 Pet 1:4). God's examples of love, given to us in his inspired word and demonstrated in the

---

7. Kirkpatrick, *Cambridge Bible*.

life of Christ, provides the light in which we are to walk. God is love, the Son (Jesus) demonstrated superior love toward us by his sacrificial death and resurrection, and the love of God is shed abroad in our hearts by the Holy Spirit (Rom 5:5). God's love has saturated us. What more do we need in order to display the love of God? "Beloved, if God so loved (*agapao*) us, we ought also to love (*agapao*) one another" (1 John 4:11).

In the way that God has loved us first, before we knew him and even while we were sinners at enmity with him, so too should we demonstrate God-type love for others. God extends his love to us, not because we deserve it or have earned it but because he is a loving God. God's divine love for us transcends our offences and imperfections. In truth, moving beyond the offenses of others is easier said than done, but if we are to love one another as God loves, unkind treatment by a brother/sister should not induce us to withdraw our love.[8] "No man hath seen God at any time. If we love (*agapao*) one another, God dwelleth in us, and his love (*agape*) is perfected in us" (1 John 4:12).

Even though we do not see God personally and physically, we can know him personally, we can study him in the Holy Spirit-breathed word of God, and we can perceive him in creation (4:12). We also experience God and grow in his love as we love one another. Love is the means through which God has designed for us to live with him and for him. "If a man say, I love (*agapao*) God, and hateth his brother, he is a liar. For he that loveth (*agapao*) not his brother whom he hath seen, how can he love (*agapao*) God whom he hath not seen?" (1 John 4:20).

The gifted Holy Spirit in the life of a redeemed person is evidence of God's love for you. Plus, we know that God sent Jesus as our sacrificial Savior so that redemption is available to all who will call upon his name. We know that God is love and as we dwell in love, God dwells in us. This knowledge of God's love for us should give us confidence that we are safe in our salvation and, therefore, we need not fear God's judgment.

---

8. Clarke, *Adam Clarke's Commentary*.

Our outworking of God's love should be demonstrated by love toward our brothers and sisters within the family of God. John proclaims that the fact that we can physically see our church family members, should motivate us to share God's love with them (4:20). If rather, we find it difficult to love someone who we see right in front of us, how genuine is it to expect that you will love God whom you cannot see. It is easier to direct our love toward someone in the seen realm than toward someone in the unseen realm. So, for one to proclaim that they love God but hate a child of God, their proclamation is evidently a lie. "And this commandment have we from him, That he who loveth (*agapao*) God love (*agapao*) his brother also" (1 John 4:21).

Following on from the previous verse, here (4:21) John reminds us of the commandment to love one another. In fact, this can be traced back to Leviticus 19:18, in which God commands Israel to not bear any grudge against a brother/sister, and to love thy neighbor as thyself. The love of God and the love of man are inseparable. One who genuinely loves God will love his brother and one who loves his brother demonstrates that he loves God and dwells in God.[9] See the logical reasoning following:

1. Every believer in the incarnation is a child of God.
2. Every child of God loves its Father.
3. Every true believer loves God.
4. Everyone who loves God loves the children of God.
5. Therefore, every believer in the incarnation loves the children of God.[10]

Set Apart from the World Unto God

Being set apart from the world unto God is also termed sanctification. As redeemed followers of Christ, we have been set apart by God as sacred. We are set apart from the carnality and immorality

---

9. Clarke, *Adam Clarke's Commentary*.
10. Kirkpatrick, *Cambridge Bible*.

of the fallen world. Sanctification is also closely related to holiness. Gradual purification from sin attraction and progressive spiritual growth should be the mark of a maturing Christian. Such maturing is also characterized by increasing purity in our love and Christlikeness. "Love (*agapao*) neither the things that are in the world. If any man love (*agapao*) the world, the love (*agape*) of the Father is not in him" (1 John 2:15).

There are numerous proofs that we have experienced in God. Our sins are forgiven, and we are adopted into the family of God. We now have a personal, ongoing relationship with God and have received the Holy Spirit as counsellor and comforter. We are empowered to live above sin and provided with armor to help protect us (Eph 6:11–18). Yet we may still be drawn in by the sensibilities of this world. The things that this fallen world offers—the lust of the flesh, the lust of the eyes, and the pride of life—are of no redeeming value to us, and they are not from God. In fact, these are things that God is opposed to. If then, this pagan world and self-centered lifestyle are the focus of your desires, you are deceived, as such worldly love excludes the love of God.

God's Love

Isn't it wonderful that we can learn about and meditate on God's love and what that means to us? And that we have the word of God and the Holy Spirit of God to teach us? As I discussed earlier, God's love is unlike the illusion of love that the pagan world portrays and promotes. God's love is holy, pure, perfect, kind, unchanging, loyal, and steadfast. Human language is limited in its ability to express the fullness of God's love. Therefore, we will continue to drink from God's supernatural words. "Behold, what manner of love (*agape*) the Father hath bestowed upon us, that we should be called the sons of God: therefore the world knoweth us not, because it knew him not" (1 John 3:1).

The love of God to man is something to behold, to contemplate on, and wonder upon. The apostle John here is in amazement, considering that the God of the universe has bestowed his love on mankind and brought us (believers) into the family of God. Yet those who will not acknowledge the love of God, bestowed in Jesus Christ to us, will not know God.

The apostle Paul in the book of Ephesians 3:16–21 prayed that God would enable us to comprehend God's love; something that is beyond our knowledge. Let us also pray along with Paul that we would grow in our understanding of the fullness of God's love. This also is something that God can grant for his glory.

> That he would grant you, according to the riches of his glory, to be strengthened with might by his Spirit in the inner man; That Christ may dwell in your hearts by faith; that ye, being rooted and grounded in love, May be able to comprehend with all saints what is the breadth, and length, and depth, and height; And to know the love of Christ, which passeth knowledge, that ye might be filled with all the fulness of God. Now unto him that is able to do exceeding abundantly above all that we ask or think, according to the power that worketh in us, Unto him be glory in the church by Christ Jesus throughout all ages, world without end. Amen. (Eph 3:16–21)

The demonstration of God's love shown for you and I, in the redeeming sacrifice of Jesus Christ, is the greatest example of love that can be given. "Greater love hath no man than this, that a man lay down his life for his friends" (John 15:13). Would you consider offering your only child, or your own life as a just sacrifice so that another could live? Jesus was a man with the feelings, emotions, and temptations common to mankind but he was also God. God the Father offered Jesus his Son to carry the burden of and to die for the sins of mankind, and Jesus the God-man was obedient to his Father because of the love of God and his love for mankind.

> In this was manifested the love (*agapao*) of God towards us, because that God sent his only begotten Son into the world, that we might live through him. Herein is love (*agape*), not that we loved (*agapao*) God, but that he loved (*agapao*) us, and sent his Son to be the propitiation for our sins. (1 John 4:9–10)

God's perfect love to man was spontaneously given, not motivated in response to our love toward him. He loved us and sent his Son to be the payment for our sins, before we loved him. Our love might be less spontaneously given, to put it mildly, but it is an ideal to be considered. The crucifixion, death, burial, and resurrection of Christ really is the climax in God's relationship with mankind. Observing this revelation of God's love, we in his image can imitate his example both back to God and out to man.

God's Love in True Believers

God's love in you and I is something to cherish. We mirror God's image when we walk in love for one another. It is by such demonstration of love that the unsaved world will know that we are genuine followers of Christ. True love will also distinguish true Christians from fake. As we've considered, the love in the world is of a different type and God's love in us is a priceless gem. "In this the children of God are manifest, and the children of the devil: whosoever doeth not righteousness is not of God, neither he that loveth (*agapao*) not his brother" (1 John 3:10).

We should know that Christ was manifested to take away our sins (1 John 3:5) and whosoever abides in Christ does not live in sin. Christ was manifested to destroy the works of the devil (1 John 3:6). If you are truly abiding in Christ, habitual sin will not be your lifestyle. Rather, opposition to sin should be the ruling principle of your life.[11] Sin should be presently remedied through confession to God and personal repentance, which results in God's forgiveness. Doing what is right in God's eyes is to be our objective and thus our Christian witness is reliant upon the demonstration of one's charity (i.e., love in action) towards members of God's family. Love for your brothers/sisters is evidence that you are a true child of God. "My little children, let us not love (*agapao*) in word, neither in tongue; but in deed and in truth" (1 John 3:18).

---

11. Kirkpatrick, *Cambridge Bible*.

We may speak loving words to another but if we stop short of fulfilling those words with action then our professions of love and humane disposition are ingenuous. If we have the resources and the ability to give to a need but we restrain our compassion, then our pleasant words are pretentious. The fulfillment of loving in word is to love in deed and in truth. "And this is his commandment, That we should believe on the name of his Son Jesus Christ, and love (*agapao*) one another, as he gave us commandment" (1 John 3:23).

When we then love in word, deed, and truth, we can have confidence before God; a clear conscience. God knows our motives and the genuineness of our actions. Through the Holy Spirit he will convict us of any misdeeds, lead us into truth, and counsel us. Believing in the gospel of Christ—in Christ's righteous sacrifice for our sins—is our only source of justification and righteousness before God. Consequently, God commands us to believe in Jesus Christ because he (i.e., Father, Son, and Holy Spirit) loves us indeed. The second commandment here, to love one another, is enabled by our obedience to the first (i.e., belief in Christ). Furthermore, understand that you who keep God's commandments dwell in God and God dwells in you. A wonderful quote by F.B. Meyer is fitting here. With relevance to our love for another, Meyer said, "Love is not measured by the expressions of the lip or the emotion of the heart, but by the extent to which we will do or suffer."[12] "He that loveth (*agapao*) not knoweth not God; for God is love (*agape*)" (1 John 4:8).

A person who does not show charity and does not share love by action is not acting as the God of love wills. Therefore, they are not displaying evidence of knowing God. In fact, earlier in chapter 4, John warns us that not every person who claims to be of God is truly a Christian. The test of the Spirit that leads them is whether they confess that Jesus has come in the flesh. Anything less than this specific confession is inspired by an antichrist spirit.

Those who know God will understand that Christ has overcome the antichrist spirit and thus greater is the Spirit of God in

12. Meyer, *Day by Day*.

Christ followers than the spirit of the heathen world. Accordingly, we can and should love one another as God loves. Our charity for the family of God proves that we are born again (i.e., our spiritual birth) and that we have an intimate, experiential relationship with God.[13]

While God is holy, just, merciful, and righteous, God specifically identifies with love (e.g., God is love). Those who do not love are not identifying with the divine nature of our God nor demonstrating that they know him. "And we have known and believed the love (*agape*) that God hath to us. God is love (*agape*); and he that dwelleth in love (*agape*), dwelleth in God, and God in him" (1 John 4:16).

It has been revealed to mankind that God sent his Son into the world to be the propitiation for our sins and that the redeemed of Christ (his elect) might live through him. Who then will live through him? Whosoever shall confess that Jesus is the Son of God, God dwells in him, and he in God (1 John 4:15). A sincere confession of faith in Christ is our key to salvation.

We have known or have come to know and have believed that God has loved us and demonstrated his love to us by sending his Son as Savior. God is love; consequently, those who dwell in love (i.e., to and from God and his body of believers) experience the presence of God. The words of Jesus recorded in John 17:26 further indicate the love of God (the Father, the Son, and the Holy Spirit) within us as followers of Christ:

> And I have declared unto them thy name, and will declare it: that the love (*agape*) wherewith thou hast loved (*agapao*) me may be in them, and I in them. (John 17:26)
>
> We love (*agapao*) him, because he first loved (*agapao*) us. (1 John 4:19)

Our recognition of the astounding love of God in us gives Christians confident assurance that we are the redeemed children of God, heirs of God, and joint heirs with Jesus Christ. So, there is no reason for us to live with servile or guilty fear of God's

---

13. Radmacher et al., *NKJV Study Bible*.

judgment, as we are the saved elect of God. However, appreciating the majesty of God should embody us with a rightful awe and reverential fear.

In truth, God first loved us, prior to our conversion and while we were still sinners. Therefore, God's love for us is the genesis of our love for him. Plus, his love shed abroad in our hearts has fuelled love in us (Rom 5:5). "Whosoever believeth that Jesus is the Christ is born of God: and every one that loveth (*agapao*) him that begat loveth (*agapao*) him also that is begotten of him" (1 John 5:1).

Only by faith in Jesus Christ, the Son of God, the anointed one, do we obtain spiritual birth. True salvific faith is contingent on our belief that God/Elohim (the Father) sent Jesus (the Son) to be our Savior. In fact, Jesus is God and man, Messiah, Lord, prophet, priest, and King. True love is displayed by our love indeed toward God (JEHOVAH) who begat Jesus Christ, his only begotten Son. Our love of God and love for the children of God is evident by our keeping of God's commandments. For the faithful, God's commandments are not grievous, as it is by faith that we overcome the world and worldliness.

Assurance in God

When conversion to Christianity is genuine, one can be assured of their salvation and that God's power and love can keep one unto heavenly glorification. Only one's genuine, freewilled renouncement of Christ can lead to true apostasy. The process of sanctification (i.e., purification to Christlikeness) in the life of a believer is a work of the Holy Spirit of God and the word of God. God does not leave us to fight on our own; his presence and love remain with us. Therefore, abide in him as he abides in you. "Herein is our love (*agape*) made perfect, that we may have boldness in the day of judgment: because as he is, so are we in this world" (1 John 4:17).

Herein is love, that God loved us first by sending his son into the world to rescue us. Whosoever will confess that Jesus is the Son of God, God dwells in him and he in God. We know that we dwell in him, and he in us, by the Holy Spirit given to us. If we then love one another, God's love is perfected in us. Herein is love made perfect, when the love of God through the Spirit of God saturates our body, soul and spirit; when the love of God emanates through us to the family of God.

As Jesus is, so are we in the world. Our assurance of salvation is not an assumption. We are the righteousness of God in Christ through faith and the sum of righteousness is love (1 John 3:14). All that belongs to Christ belongs to us by perfect imputation (justification) and progressive impartation (sanctification).[14] Jesus is pure, holy, and loving and we are being progressively made like him to practically live out that righteousness and holiness.[15] We are sanctified, being sanctified, and will be perfectly sanctified, like Christ, when we see him face to face. "There is no fear in love (*agape*); but perfect love (*agape*) casteth out fear: because fear hath torment. He that feareth is not made perfect in love (*agape*)" (1 John 4:18).

A believer's mature understanding of God's *agape* love will remove any fear (terror and/or torment) of God's judgment.[16] As we are now partakers of the Spirit of God, we have the divine approbation for justification and peace in God.[17] Hence, your trust in God's promises in the word of God, as the arbiter of truth, will negate any arguments to the contrary. Trepidation and the love of God are incompatible. Therefore, love without fear. God's love is perfect.

So What?

The love of God is perfected in us by his Holy Spirit, by the word of God, and by our charity within the family of God. Our love in action for each other displays that we are born again, and that

14. Brown et al., *Commentary*.
15. Clarke, *Adam Clarke's Commentary*.
16. Radmacher et al., *NKJV Study Bible*.
17. Clarke, *Adam Clarke's Commentary*.

God's love is shed abroad in our heart. As redeemed believers and elect children of God, we have been set apart from the ways of the heathen world unto God himself and for his purposes. As distinct from the illusion of love portrayed in the heathen world, God's love is holy, pure, perfect, kind, unchanging, loyal, and steadfast. God's love for the lost and the redeemed elect is demonstrated in John 3:16: "For God so loved the world that he gave his only begotten Son, that whosoever believes in him should not perish but have eternal life." Moreover, when we were without strength, in due time, Christ died for the ungodly (Rom 5:6). Hence, while we were still sinners (enemies of God), Christ died for us (Rom 5:8). We, the redeemed, have therefore been justified through faith in the blood of Christ and saved from just wrath (Rom 5:9). We can be assured that God who has drawn us to himself by his Holy Spirit, has chosen and redeemed us into the family of God through faith in Christ, and will keep us through faith onto glorification (John 6:44; Eph 1:4; Rom 8:30).

In my next book (volume 2), I will continue to explore and expound on true love as it is inspired and written in other books of the Bible. I know that we have much to learn about God's love to mankind, our love to God, and our love to each other. I am finding that as I analyze the text and context of Scripture, I am led down unpremeditated paths. This is a blessing to me, and I pray that it is a blessing to you too. May the Holy Spirit gift us with a greater capacity to comprehend and walk in God's love.

BIBLIOGRAPHY

Andrews, Edward D. *Calvinism vs. Arminianism: The Bible Answers*. Cambridge, OH: Christian, 2022.

Aquinas, Thomas. *Summa Theologica*. In *On Prayer and The Contemplative Life*. Moral Theology, n. d.

Brown, David, et al. *A Commentary, Critical, Experimental, and Practical on the Old and New Testaments: Acts–Revelation, vol. VI*. E-Sword version 13.0.0 ed. Glasgow, UK: William Collins, Sons and Company, 1802–80.

Clarke, Adam. *Adam Clarke's Commentary on the Bible*. E-Sword version 13.0.0 ed. Boston: Beacon Hill, 1826.

Dockery, David. *Holman Concise Bible Commentary*. L. B. S. F. Corporation., Ed. 38.1.2 ed. Nashville: Broadman and Holman, 1998.

Easton, Matthew George. *Illustrated Bible Dictionary and Treasury of Biblical History, Biography, Geography, Doctrine, and Literature*. E-Sword version 13.0.0 ed. New York: Harper and Brothers, 1893.

Kirkpatrick, Alexander Francis. *The Cambridge Bible for Schools and Colleges*. E-Sword version 13.0.0 ed. Cambridge, UK: Cambridge University Press, 1907–42.

Koiter, Ian, W. K. "Apostasy." In *The Lexham Bible Dictionary*, edited by John D. Barry et al. Bellingham, WA: Lexham, 2016.

Lewis, C. S. *The Four Loves*. Boston: Mariner, 1960.

———. *The Four Loves: Storge/Affection (Part 1/4)*. London, 1957. https://www.youtube.com/watch?v=GsGh_g_PLio.

Lockyer, Herbert, ed. *Nelson's Illustrated Bible Dictionary*. L. B. S. F. Corporation., Ed. 38.1.2 ed. Nashville: Thomas Nelson, 1996.

Meyer, F. B. *Through the Bible Day by Day: Commentary on 1 John 3:23*. E-Sword version 13.0.0 ed. American Sunday-School Union, 1918.

Orr, James. *International Standard Bible Encyclopedia*. Vol. 3. Chicago: Howard-Severance, 1915.

Radmacher, Earl D., et al. *NKJV Study Bible: New King James Version*. L. B. S. F. Corporation., Ed. 38.1.2 ed. Nashville: Thomas Nelson, 2007.

Strong, James. *Enhanced Strong's Lexicon*. New York: World, 1995.

Tozer, A. W. *Knowledge of the Holy*. New York: Harper and Row, 1961.

———. *The Pursuit of God*. Cambridge, OH: Christian, 1948.

www.ingramcontent.com/pod-product-compliance
Lightning Source LLC
LaVergne TN
LVHW051708080426
835511LV00017B/2790